A Warrior's Life

Jerry Williams

ISBN:0-9983115-0-2

ISBN-13:978-0-9983115-0-0

DEDICATION

This devotional is dedicated to all the men and women who have given up their lives for the sake of the Gospel. May you receive from the Lord a hundred-fold in this life and in the life to come, life everlasting. Thank you for your service to our Commander, King Jesus!

The Lord is a Warrior!
The LORD is His
Name! Exodus 15:3

CONTENTS

Preface

For I know the plans that I have for you, declares the LORD, plans for welfare and not for calamity to give you a future and a hope. Jeremiah 29:11

Within the heart of every human being lies an unseen eternal seed of destiny carefully deposited therein by the only True Creator and God of all. I am convinced this untouchable, invisible seed of destiny continuously speaks to each of us drawing and calling us onward and upward to a life we cannot live apart from heaven's intervention. As the children of God (those who repent and confess Jesus as their personal LORD!) we are the chosen conduits whereby the will of our Father in heaven is accomplished in the earth through the power of His indwelling Holy Spirit. What a calling! What a destiny! Therefore, it doesn't matter how menial the task we are called to accomplish may seem in this realm. We are a royal priesthood chosen to be His ambassadors carrying out His bidding for His pleasure and praise throughout all creation. All we are required to do is humbly draw near to Him, acknowledge He alone is Worthy and Wise, then quietly listen until we undeniably hear His voice calling us toward His design and destiny for each of our lives. If we will listen, then He will certainly lead us down the straight and narrow path. *For as many as are led by the Spirit of God, these are the sons of God.* Romans 8:14

Sadly, history stands as an undeniable witness that the majority of those created in the image of God never come to know or embrace their God appointed destiny. The god of this present world darkness (Satan) has blinded the eyes (minds) of the naïve and unbelieving. It is inconceivable to me that anyone would deny the reason for their existence, but it happens on a world wide scale every day. Do you know why God created you? Do you know what His purpose and destiny is for your life? Do you realize God created YOU to be His vessel wherein that which is deemed 'impossible' among men would take place through your life on a daily basis? God says you are fearfully and wonderfully made. Do you believe that?

But Jesus looked at them and said to them, with men this is impossible, but with God all things are possible. Matthew 19:26

I have often been given the opportunity to speak into the lives of many of God's captains (ministers) and under the unction of the Holy Spirit encourage and challenge them to realize God has appointed them to be ministers of the 'impossible'. Think about it. If all we accomplish through our lives are those things which are 'possible' among men, then it has no potential to ever reflect anything God size, and most often is covered with nothing more than the fingerprints of our own finite abilities. I've heard it said many times, *It's not about our ability, but about our availability*. Does your heart not stir within you when reading, *they shall mount up with wings as eagles*? Countless people have told you all of your life, *You can't fly*. Don't believe them! God created us to do the impossible! When was the last time you were facing a mountain of impossible circumstances, then you cried out for God's help and something unmistakably God size began to happen? Can you remember how God suddenly awakened your spirit and caused you to rise up and boldly proclaim, *Mountain be gone in the name of Jesus,* and it was gone?

Now faith is the substance of things hoped for, the evidence of things not seen. Hebrews 11:1

But without faith it is impossible to please Him, for he who comes to God must believe that He is, and that He is a rewarder of those who diligently seek Him. Hebrews 11:6

By the grace of God from the moment I was born again I have always been a God chaser who has lived with a sense of purpose and destiny. I can take no credit or praise for this because even the passion to pursue this destiny has been given to me by my heavenly Father and kept ablaze within my heart by the indwelling Holy Spirit. Furthermore, the Lord has filled the days of my life with a continuous stream of 'mighty men of valor' who have faithfully influenced, mentored and motivated me to be a giant slayer in a world full of men made small by giant fears. There have been many failures along the way, but He has never abandoned or disqualified me from His purpose upon my life. Thankfully, after nearly five decades of serving Him I still long to do what I have never done that I might one day see what I have never seen. I still have dreams and visions of being empowered by the Holy Spirit to do mighty exploits for our awesome God. I believe with all my heart I was created to fly, something most men my age won't even attempt! I suppose that's why I have always been quick to 'jump' in the midst of a multitude who are bound to the ground by their doubt, fear and unbelief. Although I never 'jump' without challenging those on the ground to take a leap of faith with me, I have settled in my heart I will NEVER continue dwelling with those who by choice are grounded in fear and unbelief. The prize is not on the ground, it's in the heavens where the breath of God is the constant Wind that gives me the LIFT I need to stay above the circumstances that thrive on ground level.

Throughout the years I have encountered a literal army of weary, beleaguered and defeated soldiers of God who are exhausted in their service and hopeless in their outlook for the future. Rising and staying above the circumstances is one of the primary purposes I was led to write this personal devotional. If these short stories from my life provide any resource of inspiration to any who have become worn out and weary in their journey, then to God be all the glory. If you are one of those who along life's journey have lost sight of your dreams, grown cold in your passion and have been overtaken by a spirit of weariness and fainting, then my prayer is these brief stories will be a spark God uses to ignite the fires of Hope, break asunder the dams of despair and cause the rivers of inspiration to flood over your weary heart once again. Bones Rise Up!

As you read these stories which range from my childhood days to the present (2016), I sincerely pray you will experience a renewed vision of the greatness of God's call and destiny in your life. To God alone belongs all the praise, glory and honor for what is recorded in this project. These excerpts are firsthand accounts of His greatness, power, authority and magnificent handiwork as seen through my eyes at different points along my journey. May these testimonies of His workings in and through my life give you fresh inspiration to *run the race with perseverance that is set before you*. Hebrews 12:1

I am forever...your brother in Jesus!

Jerry Williams
A Warrior of God

Introduction

The LORD is a Warrior! The LORD is His name. Exodus 15:3

In the fall of 1970 I had a radical and life changing personal encounter with Jesus Christ. Through the mercy of God I was brought to repentance, and fully acknowledged my rebellious lifestyle and desperate need for a Savior from my sin. I had been searching for the Lord for several years, but was arrogantly trying to reason with Him to accept me on my terms and conditions. In my desperation I would oftentimes say things such as, *God, if You will do this one thing for me, then I will give You my life.* Finally, I gave up all attempts to bargain with God and pleaded for His mercy and forgiveness. That night (09/01/70) I received Jesus Christ into my heart on His terms and conditions to forever be my Lord, Master and Savior. From that moment He has given me a constant passion to pursue Him and His glorious presence. By His grace He embedded within my spirit an understanding that I was called to be a warrior in His righteous army. Somehow I understood that I had been chosen and entrusted with a God appointed responsibility to help others *put on the whole armor of God.* I quickly learned that only through His power and anointing would I ever be able to stand against the destructive schemes and deadly designs of the enemy that held me in bondage for so long. I am so grateful He has given me the heart of a warrior. Amazingly even the name my mother gave me at my birth means *Warrior of God.*

Not surprisingly from that first day of my new birth in Christ until now I have experienced an almost unceasing and relentless onslaught from the enemy who has sought and schemed to destroy my reputation, health, finances, family and the ministry God has commissioned me to accomplish for His glory. Thankfully, the Holy Spirit quickly taught me that Satan's campaigning against me (and every other child of God) is designed to *steal* my hope, *kill* my confidence and *destroy* my destiny, witness and God inspired influence in the world. Through the countless battles waged in my mind and heart over these many years, the confidence, hope and trust I have gained in my Captain and King has only increased and strengthened. Many times when it seemed the darkness would overwhelm me, I found my Savior to faithfully be at my side as my Light and Salvation. Even in the midst of shameful and disgraceful failures, God has remained faithful and steadfast in His covenant and love toward me. Therefore, each and every time the enemy approaches pointing the finger at my past failures and obvious flaws I offer these words which are written on the banner of my heart:

But as for me, I will watch expectantly for the Lord; I will wait for the God of my salvation. My God will hear me. Do not rejoice over me, O my enemy. Though I fall I will rise; Though I dwell in darkness, the Lord is a light for me. Micah 7:7-8

I'm sure all of you will attest to the fact that one of the most effective resources the enemy uses to gain an advantage in our lives is our past failures. He is quick to remind us of our past sins, and the pain ushered in through them. To walk in the overcoming power of Jesus we must learn to gaze directly into the face of our past failures and see His sinless blood cleansing every stain of confessed rebellion and disobedience. When we can truly accept the love and forgiveness of God for our past rebellion and failures, then we can accept His offer to LIVE the remainder of our lives in and through Christ. Therefore, when I sense the enemy gaining ground in any area of weakness in my life I confidently lift high these words firmly placed as a banner over my mind:

Who is a God like You, who pardons iniquity and passes over the rebellious act of the remnant of His possession? He does not retain His anger forever because He delights in unchanging love. He will again have compassion on us; He will tread our iniquities under foot. Yes, You will cast all their sins into the depths of the sea. Micah 7:18-19

I know Him in Whom I have placed my life, and with absolute certainty trust Him to perfect and finish what He has started in me. In my flesh dwells no good thing, but my confidence is not in my ability to walk in what men deem as holiness, but my confidence is in Him Who shed His blood for me, heard my cries for mercy, then reached down into the dungeons of my iniquity and lifted me out of certain death placing His robes of righteousness around me.

To God be the glory! Great things He has done!
So loved He the world that He gave us His Son,
Who yielded His life an atonement for sin
And opened the life gates that all may go in!

Praise the Lord! Praise the Lord! Let the earth hear His voice!
Praise the Lord! Praise the Lord! Let the people rejoice!
O come to the Father through Jesus His Son!
And give Him the glory, great things He has done!

Are you one who is consistently derailed in your attempts to 'draw near to God'? Are you one who, try as you might, just can't seem to get past your past? I am well aware how past failures can dominate and control your mind and emotions until you are enslaved by them in the present. However, for those who acknowledge their sin, God's infinite love and mercy distributes heavenly discipline that is painful, but necessary to bring about Godly change and produce a Christ like character in us for our good and His glory.

I know, O LORD, that Your judgments are right, and that in faithfulness You have afflicted me. Psalms 119:75

Many times I have rightfully experienced the heavy burden of God's discipline, but thankfully I have never sensed He was about to cast me out of the ranks of His army or strip me of every privilege His mercy and grace have supplied to fulfill His destiny in and through my life. Yes, I know well the sting of His perfecting discipline, but have never known Him Who *knew me before I was formed in the womb* to be disappointed with choosing me to be His son. On the contrary, I know well the suffering and pain that comes from being abandoned by family as well as many of my closest brothers and sisters in Christ for my past failures. Even still, my strength and joy comes from knowing my heavenly Father has never withdrawn His support or disassociated Himself from me. Oh, how easy it is to point the finger rather than point the way to freedom when someone has miserably failed. God alone has been the unwavering faithful Voice of hope, love and confidence for my overall well-being, health and ultimate restoration. For this indescribable Gift of measureless grace and matchless love I will forever be thankful and indebted to Him. He has become and will always be my Strength, Shield, Protector, Hope, Helper, Keeper, Redeemer, Commander, Captain, Master, Savior, Lord, Physician and Friend. He alone is the continual Supply of my daily needs and the Judge and Guardian of my soul. He is my faithful Teacher and patient, loving Father. He alone has been the Source of anything praiseworthy in my life and to Him alone belongs any and all glory for whatever may be deemed valuable and honorable at any time in my life. If He is ALL that and much more for me, then He certainly will do the same and more for you.

It is my hope and prayer these daily 'nuggets' from my life will bring hope, strength, confidence, inspiration and joy to your heart that you, too, may *run the race with perseverance looking to Jesus, the Pioneer and Perfecter of our faith*, and finish the race that is set before you for His glory and praise.

Jerry Williams
Born: February 1950
Born again: September 1970

DAY 1 LIVING STONES

Then he chose for himself five smooth stones from the brook, and put them in a shepherd's bag, in a pouch which he had, and his sling was in his hand. And he drew near to the Philistine...Then David put his hand in his bag and took out a stone; and he slung it and struck the Philistine in his forehead, so that the stone sank into his forehead, and he fell on his face to the earth. So David prevailed over the Philistine with a sling and a stone. 1 Samuel 17:40, 48-50

As a young boy I lived on the western edge of Odessa, an oil boom town in the semi-desert region of West Texas. The men who worked the oil rigs were known as 'rough necks', and they truly were a hard-working, hard-living 'rough' bunch of guys. They were a harsh talking group who all seemingly had an insatiable appetite for fighting, women and beer, lots and lots of beer, especially Lone Star long neck bottled beer. I can still see in my mind's eye the ditches along the roads littered with hundreds of empty long neck bottles thrown out by the 'rough necks' traveling to and from their shift changes on the rigs. Although this created a terrible eye sore for the surrounding area, it was a continual resource for one of my favorite games while growing up. On any given weekend I would scour the south side of the ditch along FM1965 looking for a load of unbroken bottles. I would gather up at least a dozen of the discarded bottles, then head out into the nearby pasture on my grandparent's property. My mother was a single mom and had moved us into a small wood framed white house Papaw had set up in one of their pastures. We had no grass whatsoever in the yard, but instead had an abundance of dust, mesquite trees, rattlesnakes, tarantulas, red and black ants, and lots of caliche rocks everywhere. Once I had retrieved enough bottles, I would then carefully line them up in a single row leaving about three feet between each individual bottle. I would then collect a pile of rocks, back up about thirty paces and launch an imaginary assault at the oncoming enemy (the bottles). The 'war' had now begun and the otherwise useless bottles had now become a fierce and formidable enemy advancing toward my unsuspecting family inside the small white house. My only available weapon were the ubiquitous caliche rocks. It didn't take long before I learned that not just any size or shape rocks would do. I found the rocks with jagged edges didn't fly nearly as well as flatter, smoother rocks, so I would painstakingly search the pasture to find rocks that had been smoothed out from years of exposure to the harsh elements of the semi-desert like environment. Upon filling my pockets with these smaller, smoother stones, I would then return to the 'war zone' and launch my assault upon the advancing enemy.

On one particular occasion my older brother Jimmy came wandering out into the 'war zone' to see what I was doing. After a few moments of watching he asked if he could join in 'the war', too. Much to my surprise he unwisely jumped on the side of the enemy and began waging "war" against me. At first he began picking up whatever rocks were close by and started throwing them back at me. I quickly called a 'time out' to explain the rules of the game (rules I was making up on the fly). Once the rules were established and understood we took sides again and launched the 'war'. The rules that fateful day were simple: the first one to break all the opposing bottles would be declared the Victor. Of course, before the "war" could begin we each had to stockpile our arsenal (gather a bunch of rocks). As usual I carefully looked for medium sized smoother stones while my brother gathered up whatever was close no matter the size or shape. In his thinking the bigger rocks gave him a bigger chance of hitting the smaller target. Therefore, when the 'war' finally began my brother found it far more difficult to hit my bottles simply because he didn't have the right kind of weapon. It wasn't long before I had taken out several of his mighty warriors while he had miserably failed to hit a single bottle on my side. In a moment of frustration, he changed his strategy and decided to start hurling his larger, heavier, jagged-edged rocks directly at me. I easily identified and dodged these insidious attempts to bring me down as I continued eliminating his warriors one at a time. I waited patiently for the right moment, then carefully chose one of my best rocks which I had purposefully been saving to help close out the "war". Taking aim, I confidently launched the smaller, smooth stone at the enemy. This time, however, I didn't aim at the bottles, but rather took dead aim at my brother who in my mind now represented the wicked giant Goliath. As David did that day in the valley I did in the pasture letting my stone fly toward the unsuspecting giant. In less than three seconds the "war" was officially declared over as my carefully chosen weapon skillfully soared toward the giant and struck him squarely in the head. It was truly a biblical moment (so I thought) as I stood triumphantly with my hands raised in victory. My poor brother, the would-be usurper, had fallen to the ground screaming in pain. My mother wasn't nearly as excited about my victory that day as I was. Oh, for all of you who are wondering, my brother lived to fight another day.

..you also, as living stones, are being built up a spiritual house, a holy priesthood, to offer up spiritual sacrifices acceptable to God through Jesus Christ. 1 Peter 2:5

When we first give our lives to Christ and become 'born again', we are much like those bigger, bulkier stones. However, as living stones we must be willing to allow the Lord to do whatever is necessary to break off the rough, jagged edges of our hearts that we might be molded into effective warriors who might one day be "giant slayers" in God's army. Too often we ignorantly blame God for the hard things we are going through when all the while He is mercifully and necessarily smoothing out the rough edges of our lives to assure us the victory we've been praying for so long. Although I am no longer a young man, I still have a passion to be a "giant slayer" in the hand of my Savior. Whenever the Lord walks through His pastures looking for smooth living stones, I want Him to stop, pick me up out of the creek bed of life and put me in His Shepherd's pouch ready for future use. Then when the time is right, He will confidently and skillfully send me (a giant slayer in the Hand of God) directly at the head of the enemy. The gates of hell will not prevail! Anybody want to play "war" today?

David prevailed over the Philistine with a sling and a stone!

Prayer

Dear Father,

Help me to recognize and then never abandon the place of refining and preparation wherein You have lovingly led me for such a time as this. I fully accept that You are knocking the rough edges off my soul and spirit. Teach me to patiently, expectantly and joyfully allow You to do everything necessary to assure that You alone will have complete control of every aspect of my life. Do whatever it takes that one day You will place me as a living stone in Your Shepherd's pouch for Your future use. I know and accept You love me, and that You are molding and re-shaping me for my good and Your glory. I trust You, Father, and long to become a 'giant slayer' in Your hand. Amen.

The Story Behind the Song:

As a child the whole idea of playing 'war' was something I instinctively embraced, as do all children from their earliest years. The truth is we are all born into a state of perpetual WAR and live our days in a continuous spiritual WAR ZONE. For those of us who are soldiers of the cross of Christ some years the WAR is more fierce and relentless than others. One of those relentless years for me was 1996. It had truly been a year of unceasing 'warfare', especially concerning my two oldest children. During that year it became evident each of them had a serious drug problem which led one of them to become dangerously suicidal. How could this be? I was a minister of the gospel of Jesus Christ and our home was a dedicated sanctuary wherein the presence of God was sought and honored at all times. The battle and the blatant rebellion was unrelenting which wrought a heavy toll on my embattled spirit, and eventually my marriage. I became so weary from the unending onslaught I began seriously considering going AWOL from the call of God on my life and leaving the ministry. No matter where I looked all I could see was darkness, defeat and confusion. Those were incredibly lonely days for me as a father, and as a minister. It was during one of those dark, lonely days the voice of the Lord came in suddenly like a flood and spoke a stern command to my fleeting heart saying, 'Warrior, ARISE!' In that moment my eyes were opened to the bondage I had slipped into and I clearly saw myself as a prisoner of WAR. Instantaneously I cried out to the Lord for mercy, forgiveness and immediate deliverance. Then, with all my might I lifted up my voice and shouted, 'NO' straight into the face of the enemy who had so cunningly deceived me through my tattered emotions. In a moment the chains fell from my heart, I ceased being a victim and turned my focus back to being a soldier of the cross and more than a conqueror in Christ. In the moments following that glorious deliverance I picked up my guitar and the music for *Warriors Arise* began pouring out until the song was completed. The lyrics are the scriptures the Holy Spirit was speaking to my heart, as well as the command He had given me to ARISE out of my pity party and STAND in the Name and power of my COMMANDER and KING, JESUS! Some songs take years to complete, but *Warriors Arise* was written that very day and by the grace of God continues to encourage weary and embattled soldiers of Christ to this day.

Warriors Arise

(Title song from Warriors Arise Project, music and lyrics written by Jerry Williams)

The weapons of our warfare
Are not of this world, they're powerful
Tearing down the strongholds of hell!
We do not war according to our flesh
We fight against all wickedness
We are the enemies of hell.

We're standing in the armor of our God
We are protected by the blood
Of Jesus Christ our Lord!
And even though we face the power of death
We will not give in to the flesh, we are the warriors of God!

Chorus
Holy Warriors arise and storm the gates of hell.
Stand fearless in the Savior's power
For we will overcome, we'll conquer
Hell will not prevail!

We'll stand and fight the fight of faith
United in this evil day against the rulers of this world.
We'll follow without hesitation, wear the helmet of salvation
Holding up His holy Word!

We're soldiers of a different kind
We've chosen to give up our lives that we might live forevermore.
We've been given the authority to overcome the enemy
Through the name of Christ our Lord!

Chorus

Bridge
Hell will not! NO! Hell will not! NO! Hell will not prevail!
Hell will not! NO! Hell will not! NO! Hell will not prevail!

Chorus

DAY 2 WHO SAID MEN CAN'T FLY?

But those who wait on the LORD Shall renew their strength; They shall mount up with wings like eagles. Isaiah 40:31

As a young boy I had one particular dream that kept occurring over and over until I was well into my twenties. My earliest remembrance of this dream was when I was only five or six years old, but it was so realistic it eventually changed and molded the way I thought. Because of this amazing re-occurring dream I became convinced I was created to 'fly'. Each time I dreamed I was flying it was always without the help of any man made wings or any other apparatus. I just needed to believe it was possible, spread out my arms and jump.

When the dream first started occurring, most of the time I would take flight to escape some older, bigger bully who was chasing me at school or in my neighborhood. What an incredible sense of freedom to simply spread my arms and effortlessly soar away from the approaching enemy and certain disaster. As I grew older the dream became even more vivid and evolved to the point wherein I began actually taking flight to rescue others who were in various kinds of peril or danger. This dream was so remarkably real it created an ever intensifying belief in my mind that I really was created to fly. Consequently, I began looking for creative ways to put into action my firm belief that I was supposed to fly. It wasn't long before my belief in the dream motivated me to ACTION. My first leaps of faith were meager attempts from such things as elevated porches, brick fences, small trees, etc.

Eventually I began climbing to higher, loftier places (usually the roof of our house, even higher fences and trees) that would give me a greater chance to fulfil my destiny and finally take flight. I can't remember ever climbing to one of these lofty positions and then choosing to not jump. I always took the leap of faith, no matter the consequence because my FAITH WAS BIGGER THAN MY FEAR! My anticipation and expectation were always so elevated I would fearlessly launch myself forward, all the while flapping my arms believing that would be the glorious moment I would finally fly.

After several painfully unsuccessful and unhealthy attempts I stopped jumping for a while. But even after multiple embarrassing crashes, the dream still wouldn't die! So, rather than using common sense and giving up on what everyone else assured me was crazy and totally impossible, I became more determined to find newer and more creative ways to one day see my dream become reality. Then one day, years after that first night I dreamed I could fly, I discovered what I was convinced would be my launch pad to success! It was on a day we were visiting my grandparents who lived out of town that I discovered my long awaited ladder to success. Jack had his beanstalk, and now I had my grandfather's 70 foot high tripod TV antenna tower extending majestically above the tops of the old elm trees that surrounded their country home. I couldn't believe I hadn't seen or thought of it before.

After spending a few moments with my grandparents I quietly made my way outside making sure no one was paying any attention to what I might be doing outside. It was a windy spring day and the sound of the wind rustling through the leaves of the old weathered elm trees sounded like a heavenly chorus singing Alleluia in preparation for my upcoming victorious flight. I fearfully, but excitedly climbed up my grandfather's antenna tower until I was several feet higher than the tops of the giant elm trees that created a spectacular canopy over the green shingled roof of my grandparent's house. I can still remember the feeling of the tower swaying slightly back and forth in the wind, something you couldn't see from the ground. As I carefully turned around positioning myself facing outward with the tower pressing into my back, I then faced my greatest fear and came face to face with a crisis of FAITH. Suddenly everything within me began questioning if I was really meant to fly. As FEAR sought to grip my mind and paralyze my FAITH I quickly set my mind squarely back on the DREAM. It didn't take but a moment after recounting the DREAM that I dispelled the wicked intruder (FEAR) and refocused on the purpose at hand. I lifted up my head and took the whole amazing scene in as I had at that point climbed higher than I had ever been in my life. It was truly exhilarating! Then I reminded myself I hadn't climbed this high just to prove my dreams couldn't come true. NO! I was there to see the impossible take place. I was there to put my FAITH into ACTION. I was CREATED TO FLY, and this was the day I was going to finally SOAR LIKE THE EAGLES!

I still have no memory of what took place in the next few seconds. The only memory I have is lying on the ground looking up through the branches wondering what had just happened. Thankfully, that was my final attempt at physically flying. I'm not certain how long it took after that day before the dreams quit occurring, but the impact and realness of those incredibly wonderful dreams still lingers with me to this day. I still have an intense desire to soar like the eagle and swoop down to rescue the perishing from impending danger and certain destruction. One thing I have learned is this:

You will never take the leap if you don't first dream the dream.

Throughout my lifetime I've always carried with me the label of being a radical. The truth is I don't feel very radical the majority of the time. I'm sure most of you can relate to that feeling, can't you? However, even though I'm now much older, I still live with an insatiable hunger to be more than I've ever been, do more than I've ever been capable of doing, and see more than I've ever seen done in and through my life. If that's what it means to be radical, then may I be even more so in the days to come. I have to ask, am I really that radically different than most of you? I really wonder. It's always amazed me that so few of those I've known through the years still have this same drive and hunger today. Have you ever dreamed you could fly? If so, do you still long to spread your arms and soar like the eagle? Please don't tell me you're one of those who were a radical as a young man or woman, but over time slowly evolved into a stagnant, immovable conservative in your later years. How did this happen? Did you lose your ability to dream dreams that take you beyond your physical and mental capabilities to a place where the impossible is commonplace? Has it been so long you've forgotten what it was like to dream you could fly? Is there still a glimmer of hope that you could still believe it's possible for YOU to do the impossible and FLY?

Even though I failed a thousand times in all my attempts to physically fly, and even though I was hurt or injured on many occasions through the process, heaven is my witness that I will not quit dreaming, never quit believing, and never quit trying to do the impossible. It doesn't matter that the majority of those I encounter tell me all the things that aren't possible! I refuse to listen or heed the voices of those who base their beliefs on that which they can see, taste, smell, feel or hear. I believe and am convinced men were created in the image of God to one day do the impossible and FLY like the eagle.

Blow wind! Blow! Lift me from my place
High above normalcy, high above the graves
Of other men who lost their dreams
and long have since forgot
That God created every man
To fly on wings of Hope!

Let me offer this challenge to each of you who are being stirred in your heart to once again believe in the unbelievable and expect the unexpected:

Dream the dreams you did at first,
And slay the giants of this earth
Dare to soar on wings of hope
That in the end you will be known
First in hell as a "Man of God",
Then in the hearts of all who trod
Upon the path you first explored
When you dared to let God in you be Lord!

Does anyone want to go over this afternoon to my grandparents with me? I would love to show you how my grandfather's tripod TV antenna tower sways in the wind the higher up you go. I double dog triple dare you!

Prayer

O my heavenly Father,

Remove all fear of the unknown out of the depths of my heart. Give me eyes that gaze continually upward and are never distracted by the momentary circumstances surrounding me on every side. I believe, but help me in my unbelief. Overwhelm my ever-present weaknesses with the knowledge of Your surpassing greatness and power that dwells within me. Awaken my spirit to dream again! Unite my divided heart so that in the days to come I will be an instrument of Your deliverance to men who are buried beneath the fodder of forgotten or mediocre dreams and man size accomplishments. Cause me to be an inspiration to others I meet along the way that they, too, might become motivated to believe in the impossible. Fill me with a supernatural and steadfast confidence whenever I feel the winds of circumstance trying to sway me from believing You. Open the eyes of my heart to see that I truly was created to fly. In the name of Jesus, the One Who flew first! Amen.

Some glad morning when this life is o'er I'll fly away!
To a land on God's celestial shore I'll fly away!
I'll fly away, O glory! I'll fly away!
When I die, hallelujah bye and bye, I'll fly away!

<u>The Story Behind the Song:</u>

Just prior to my writing the song *Dreams* I was at a major crossroads in my life needing to make a very difficult decision whether to throw caution to the wind and chase my 'dream' or maintain a steady course in life. Although the 'dream' was God size, pursuing it offered no tangible financial assurances for the immediate future while maintaining my present position as an associate pastor offered my family continued stability and security. As I wrestled with what direction to take, the Lord powerfully spoke to my heart saying He had created me to 'fly'.

In the moments that followed He further challenged me that as His Ambassador I was called to be a minister of the 'impossible'. In short, I was wrestling with maintaining what was 'possible' or taking a LEAP of faith and pursuing what almost everyone else said was an 'impossible dream'. It was in the midst of this personal crisis of faith the Lord gave me the song, *Dreams*. In those moments I was reminded again of the sheer elation I felt every time I awoke from dreaming I could FLY.

Soon the fear of taking a LEAP of faith disappeared and a joyful expectation for what God was about to do settled in my heart. By the grace of God I did take that LEAP of faith and the 'impossible dream' became reality. I pray God gives each of you the courage to 'dream', but also to trust Him to passionately pursue that God breathed impossible dream until it becomes a reality to the glory of our awesome God.

Dreams

Music and lyrics written by Jerry Williams

Have you ever dreamed of times you felt yourself flying...
And you thought you had the freedom of the skies?
It seemed as though to wake was almost like dying
For the pleasure of your dream had flown away?

Chorus 1
But lift up your eyes and see the Light of the world is shining in
Filling your heart with love and freedom
So who needs (wants) to fly?

Lord, I want to dream of the day that You will be coming
And You'll meet with all Your children in the clouds
That will be a day when waking will be joyful
That will be a time for singing praise out loud!

Chorus 2
For all of my hopes and dreams
Have all come true because of Him
Jesus, the Word of God is living!
Praise God I'm alive!

So lift up your eyes and see
The Light of the world is shining in
Filling your heart with love and freedom
So who needs (wants) to fly?

It will come about after this that I will pour out My Spirit on all mankind. And your sons and daughters will prophesy,
Your old men will dream dreams, Your young men will see visions.
Joel 2:28

DAY 3 GONE FISHING

Then He said to them, "Follow Me, and I will make you fishers of men." Matthew 4:19

As I extracted and released the helpless grasshopper from the pool, I imagined in my mind hearing it say 'thank you' as it triumphantly flew away. Suddenly, in an instant I was unexpectedly translated back into a time in my life when things were much simpler and far less complicated. From deep in the coffers of my mind came forth a wonderful memory of the joyful face of Grandpa Sherwood as he was teaching us how to catch grasshoppers one early summer afternoon just outside Shamrock, Texas. I was only four or five years old and we were visiting Grandma and Grandpa for a few days so they could get to know us better. I didn't really understand all that was going on, but what I did know was that my mother had just married Gene Williams, and the Sherwood's were his grandparents. So, now I had a new step dad and got new grandparents in the deal, too. What I had no way of knowing at that time was how much my new grandparents would prove to be a vital part of God's destiny in my life not too many years later.

From the moment I met Grandpa Sherwood I thought he was amazing. It might have had something to do with him telling us just after we arrived that he was taking us fishing the next morning. I had never gone fishing before, but after hearing that I was so excited I kept following him everywhere like a little puppy following its new owner. Not long after we had spent some time getting to know Grandma Sherwood, Grandpa took us outside to start making preparations for the next morning's fishing trip. I had no idea that the ubiquitous grasshoppers which were a constant plague to the farmers would be our secret super bait. The first thing Grandpa did was give each of us a glass jar with a lid. Then he showed us how to punch holes in the lid to let air in so our super bait wouldn't die overnight.

Then Grandpa loaded us all up in his old car and drove to a nearby field that was overgrown with grass and weeds that towered over my head. In only seconds he started snatching jumbo grasshoppers out of the tall grass. I still can remember the sound of him laughing as we stood staring in awe at how easily he caught the unsuspecting grasshoppers. It wasn't long before he had shown each of us how to do the same thing, then turned us loose to fill our jars with the bounty of the field. The whole time we were snatching up the grasshoppers Grandpa kept laughing and telling us how wonderful the next morning was going to be fishing in a close by farm pond. Over and over he kept repeating how great the next morning's fishing was going to be because the Lord had supplied so many really big and juicy grasshoppers.

I had no idea at the time this would be my first and only fishing trip with this gentle and amazing man. Although he was already in his late seventies, at that time he was still climbing and trimming trees for people who lived around the town, and did it all with a handsaw. Amazing!

When we returned from catching what Grandpa Sherwood described as a bumper crop of grasshoppers, Grandma Sherwood told everyone she was so sure we were going to catch a lot of fish the next morning we would be having a big fish fry the following afternoon. My mind was racing so fast I could hardly wait to go to bed later that night. My imagination was filled with thoughts of adventure and excitement which made it really difficult to fall asleep. It seemed as though I had just dozed off when Grandpa came in with a boisterous voice proclaiming, 'Get up! Get up! Anyone want to go fishing?' It was 4:30 in the morning, a time I can honestly say I had never before willingly even thought about getting up. That didn't matter on this morning, though! I bounced out of bed in anticipation of the great adventure that awaited. Of course Grandma was already in the kitchen frying up bacon and eggs and baking homemade biscuits so we would all have a good breakfast before leaving. Ahhh, the smell of those homemade biscuits and jelly still makes my mouth water even to this day.

As soon as we finished eating and had all brushed our teeth, we headed out to the old hand built wooden garage that looked to me more like a magical dwelling place for some mystical creature you would only see in a fairy tale. As Grandpa swung the old, rickety doors open, he then reached up for something hidden high in the rafters. With a gleam in his eye he pulled down several long, well used cane poles. 'Here are your fishing poles', he excitedly exclaimed. He stopped long enough to take a few moments to show each of us how to use the old cane poles, then said, 'Let's go get 'em'. By now it was nearly 6:00 a.m. as we all excitedly loaded up into his old black car. In less than ten minutes we were well outside the city limits when Grandpa suddenly pulled off on the side of the road, cut the engine off and said, 'We're here! Everybody out!'

As we jumped out and looked around we couldn't see anything but farmland and trees. He said not to worry because the secret pond was not more than a stone's throw on the other side of the fence. We all grabbed out cane poles and jars of grasshoppers (which were all still alive), then followed Grandpa over to a nearby barbed wire fence. He gently pulled on the two middle strands of the rusty wire until there was plenty of space for us to safely step through onto the other side. Just ahead was a large stand of elm trees completely keeping out of sight a beautiful little farm pond. As we made our way through the trees suddenly we were standing on the banks of what I thought was the most beautiful place I had ever been before. Then Grandpa joyfully said, 'Take out your jars of grasshoppers and let's get started.' Grandpa then taught each of us how to attach the grasshopper to the hook and then swing the line into the water. In a flash we were all ready and bobbers were splashing into the water. Grandpa then quietly turned to me and said, 'follow me'. He purposefully moved me several yards down the bank well away from the others, then began slowly wading out into the pond. I timidly followed him, cane pole in tow, out into the cold water.

The first thing that fascinated me was how the bottom of the pond felt under my now bare feet. Soon Grandpa said, 'That's far enough, son'. I was now waist high in the water, something none of the others were instructed to do. Grandpa helped me throw the line out as far as it would go, then said something I didn't understand at first: 'In just a moment your bobber will start to go under, but be patient until the fish takes it completely out of sight.' He hadn't anymore gotten those words out of his mouth when the bobber started sliding sideways in the water. I wanted to yank that old cane pole with all my might, but he said, 'Wait! Wait! Wait!' I couldn't believe how far the bobber kept moving sideways, but then all of a sudden it was gone. Suddenly I heard him joyfully shout, 'Now, son! Now!' I pulled on that old pole with all my might and the biggest fish I had ever hooked began to pull back. What an awesome feeling! It was only a few seconds and I was triumphantly standing on the bank next to the first fish I had ever caught. I was so excited I didn't want him to help the others, but stay and help me catch another one. He laughed and said, 'You know what to do now. Get back out there and catch another one.'

We all caught fish nonstop until we eventually ran out of grasshoppers. At that point we packed up the cane poles, took off the remainder of our clothes and went swimming in the creek that flowed into the pond. While we swam in the cool creek water Grandpa cleaned the fish for Grandma's afternoon fish fry. As soon as Grandpa had finished cleaning the fish we headed back home just in time for an early lunch. We nearly toppled Grandma over as we ran into the kitchen to tell her of our day. I still can see the smile on her face as she made lunch for all of us. That evening we had the big 'fish fry' and ate all the fish we caught that morning. To this day I don't think I've ever tasted fish that were anywhere close to being as good as what we caught and ate that day.

I'm a Grandfather now and am waiting patiently for the day I get to take my grandkids fishing. Sadly, I don't have any old cane poles, but I still remember everything Grandpa taught me over sixty years ago. Many of the things I've learned and held onto through the years can be traced back to those special and rare days I had the great honor of hanging out with Grandpa Sherwood. Many of the godly qualities I learned from that gracious and humble man are the very things I am endeavoring to pass on to others I meet along the way, especially other ministers and leaders who have become bogged down in the 'work' of the ministry and have long since forgotten how to simply and joyfully 'catch fish'.

Today there are thousands of different gadgets being promoted as the latest, greatest 'must have' thing to have in your tackle box to catch fish. Amazingly they are all man-made objects resembling something God made a long time ago. Man's inventions proclaim to give us the latest edge on fishing when the Lord has proclaimed He has already given us *everything we need for life and godliness.* (2 Peter 1:3) He has already provided all the necessary tools we need and as our Wise Heavenly Father stands patiently ready to teach us how to be the best fishers of men we can ever be. All it takes is a few moments watching Him joyfully show us how to do it. After all, we are His kids.

Far too many pulpits today are filled with ministers who have ventured into the warehouse of man's inventions and are spending far too much time perusing the unlimited number of ways an army of earthly manufacturers tell you how to catch fish. We don't need the latest, greatest gadgets or gimmicks to catch fish! God has already abundantly provided more than enough grasshoppers as well as tried and true cane poles. By His design we are re-created *(a new creation in Christ)* to be the extension of His hand (the line) which carries the bait (the Gospel) to those incredibly hungry fish (the world). All we have to do is wade out into the water with Him, cast out the bait, then wait until the bobber is taken out of sight. If we will do this, then we will certainly bring home the greatest stringer of fish we've ever caught.

I have heard it said time after time over the last decade that being in the ministry has become extremely difficult in these trying times. Is that really true, or have we unknowingly gotten our eyes off the Master Fisherman and His way of catching fish? I believe there are many sincere fishers of men who have unknowingly ended up in total chaos and confusion while traversing the endless isles of untried products that have yet to catch a single fish. Maybe it's time for us all to get our eyes off the product and back on the joyful face of the One Who stands ready to say, 'Wake up! It's time to go fishing!'

Prayer

Dear heavenly Father,

Help me to balance the wonders and availability of technology with the simplicities of the gospel of Your Son, Jesus Christ. I am soberly aware of the dangers of trying to reach people through my talent, gifts and abilities rather than simply sharing the unconditional love You have for every individual I encounter along the way. Please forgive me. May I never again replace the necessity of telling others about Jesus with trying to overwhelm or reach them through the use of man-made products or my own productions. Thank You for all the inspiration You give me to produce music, messages and other materials for You and Your glory. Thank You for all the talents and abilities You have entrusted to me. I once again recommit every gift and ability to You for Your use and pleasure. I relinquish all rights and authority to do with those gifts what I desire and fully acknowledge that my life is no longer my own, but Yours to do with as You will and please. Lead and guide me to the place wherein I will catch many men for Your glory and praise. Amen.

The Story Behind the Song:

Sometimes Life comes at you so hard it's easy to get your eyes off the 'main thing' and focus on the confusion. That's especially true when trying to operate a ministry to the glory of God. It was the early 1990's and we were in the midst of a season in the ministry I often referred to as a 'staff infection'. Unknowingly our ministry offices had become infiltrated and infected by a couple of individuals who came to us with personal agendas secretly hoping to advance their own ministries rather than seeking to simply be servants willing to do whatever was needed. No matter how much I spoke with them personally their eyes were on a bigger prize. Finally, in desperation I cried out to the Lord asking Him to literally flood our entire staff (beginning with me) with His presence, conviction, power and cleansing, and GET US BACK TO THE BASICS OF LOVING AND LIVING FOR HIM. By the grace of God within a few days He answered my prayers and a revival broke out among our staff. In the days following this God size breakthrough God gave me the song *Mighty River* which speaks of the joy and simplicity that comes from being in the flow of the River of God's delights. What a joy it was later that year to have several of the staff come to the studio and actually sing background vocals on the song *Mighty River* as we recorded it.

Thankfully that spirit of revival and unity continued for the next several months as everyone was blessed and honored simply to have the opportunity to work for the glory of our awesome God!

Mighty River
(Title song to Mighty River Project, music and lyrics written by Jerry Williams)

Chorus
Mighty river flow over me
Take me to the deepest part of the crystal sea
There cleanse and break everything unclean in me
Mighty river flow over me

If you stand on the bank of the river at night and listen to the water roll
It doesn't seem to take such a very long time
For the water to take control
It will soothe your heart, it will ease your mind,
It will rest your weary soul
All it's gonna take is just a little time to let the water roll

Chorus

If you stay for a while the river will tell you
Things you've never been told.
For the very first time you'll open your eyes
And see another world
Your heart will sing! You'll want to shout
And dance unto the Lord!
And all it's gonna take is just a little time
To let the water roll...to let the water roll.

Chorus

Try to think back to the time you were young
And stood at the water's edge.
You'd skip a lot of rocks and find a few frogs
'Till the river became your friend.

It soothed your heart, it eased your mind,

Gave rest to your weary soul.
All it ever took was just a little time
To let the water roll, to let the water roll.

Chorus

Then he showed me a river of the water of life, clear as crystal, coming from the throne of God and of the Lamb. On either side of the river was the tree of life, bearing twelve kinds of fruit, yielding its fruit every month; and the leaves of the tree were for the healing of the nations. There will no longer be any curse; and the throne of God and of the Lamb will be in it, and His bond-servants will serve Him; they will see His face, and His name will be on their foreheads. And there will no longer be any night; and they will not have need of the light of a lamp nor the light of the sun, because the Lord God will illumine them; and they will reign forever and ever. Revelation 22:1-5 NASU

DAY 4 OBSTACLES: BLESSINGS OR CURSE?

Consider it all joy, my brethren, when you encounter various trials, knowing that the testing of your faith produces endurance. And let endurance have its perfect result, that you may be perfect and complete, lacking in nothing. James 1:2-4 NASB

[The following testimony took place during the last few months of 2011 and carried over into most of 2012.]

Over the last few months (2011) we experienced some of the most wonderful days of ministry we've known since launching EPIC Ministries in 1998 *(not all seasons in the ministry are always so encouraging or wonderful).* Not surprisingly, we are now (2012) facing several challenging, difficult and unexpected struggles. Even so, God has given us a steadfast confidence that every 'obstacle' we are currently encountering will ultimately be used as a vehicle to bring Him greater glory in and through our lives. Therefore, we have chosen to view these momentary struggles as constant reminders God is with us, for us, in us and surrounding us with His songs and shouts of protection and deliverance. If we truly believe what He tells us, then these 'obstacles' will turn out for our good rather than our harm (Romans 8:28).

In Exodus chapters 14 and 15 we see God miraculously delivering His people by holding back the waters of the Red Sea as they cross over on dry land. As the powerful Egyptian army approaches and are at the very heels of His people, God swallows up the mighty foe in the midst of the waters. If you will remember, the children of God were being led by the Spirit of God with a cloud by day and a pillar of fire by night (Exodus 13:21). Notice carefully where God chose to lead them after this great and glorious victory. He purposefully led them into the wilderness where they found themselves without water for the next three days. When they eventually did find water, it was bitter and not fit for consumption. Do you remember how the people reacted? They murmured, grumbled and complained against Moses and the Lord.

How often after a great victory in our lives do we find ourselves in the wilderness facing 'obstacles' that in that moment seem insurmountable? After a season of great victory and many shouts of joy we must now recognize with the eyes of faith that we have been purposefully led by the Holy Spirit into a dry, thirsty place where the only water that can be found is undrinkable. Right now everything in us wants to cry out, 'How will we survive?' Oh, how easy it would be to quickly forget the bountiful blessings of God we basked in just days earlier. It's in these times we MUST remember God is the One Who has led us into this dry and difficult place. He hasn't abandoned us, but instead clearly has some greater reason for bringing us here that He knows will strengthen us in areas of lingering weakness and prepare us for what awaits us in the future. We must never forget He is our Father and has not led us down this path for our destruction, but has in His love, wisdom and mercy already provided the way of escape, deliverance and complete victory (1 Cor. 10:13). Notice that Moses didn't respond the same way as the people by murmuring against the Lord. Instead, the man of God called upon the Lord with absolute confidence and believed their deliverance was at hand. Consequently, the Lord told Moses exactly what to do, and in obedience the man of God acted upon the Word. Soon after the bitter pool was miraculously turned into pure, sweet water.

Whatever bitter pool you might be presently wading through (or seemingly drowning in) will in the same way turn sweet if you recognize and acknowledge God is with you in the midst of the trouble (Psalm 46:1). Immediately turn your murmuring and whining into trusting worship and call upon Him with a heart of confidence. Remind yourself of His promise that *all things work together for the good of those who love Him and are called according to His purpose*. You belong to Him! He Who cannot lie will honor His covenant Word and turn your bitter conditions into a triumphant well-spring, if you will acknowledge and seek Him first.

See to it that no one comes short of the grace of God; that no root of bitterness springing up causes trouble, and by it many be defiled. Hebrews 12:15 NASB

I know this all probably sounds too simple, but it's not! I can easily remember a season in the ministry when my thoughts became so embittered my entire life became a stagnant bitter pool. I had just taken a position as the youth pastor in a local church on the west side of Orlando, Florida. For three years prior to my coming to this church I had been ministering on a national platform doing revivals and crusades, but having just been married, I now needed to stay in one place so I could focus on building a healthy marriage and start a family. The staff position in Orlando seemed like a perfect fit since we had held a revival there just a year earlier and had seen over one hundred people come to Christ. The senior pastor, who had been there for many years, had always been the only full time staff member of the church other than a part time church secretary. Therefore, he had no experience working with others who were called to do the same thing he was doing in the ministry. I hadn't been there more than a week when I began believing I had made a huge mistake and was in deep trouble. The first week I was on the job the pastor called me into his office and for the two brutal hours this weary, wounded man told me everything that was wrong with 'my way' of doing things. I limped out of his office feeling devastated and confused. It would be impossible to truly express how often over the next three years I pleaded with the Lord to open any door for me to go elsewhere, but the heavens remained silent. It's not that I didn't have several opportunities to go elsewhere in the ministry, but each time an opportunity would arise the Lord emphatically made it clear I wasn't to go anywhere. During this whole 'bitter' time in my life the church amazingly grew and prospered more than at any other time in its existence. Remarkably, after only eighteen months the church had gone from approximately 200 to nearly 800 in regular attendance. One would think this would have caused things to get much better, but NOT SO! Everything continued to decay relationally between the pastor and myself until he began openly targeting me from the pulpit pointing his finger at me voicing numerous things he was displeased with in my work. Still God told me to STAY PUT! Eventually I became so deeply wounded and weary with it all I simply gave up and withdrew into a hardened impenetrable shell.

Thankfully that's not the end of the story. Had I just trusted and believed that God had led me to that place, to that man and that trouble, I would have easily seen the gaping wound in the heart and spirit of the pastor. If I hadn't been so immature and self-centered I could have immediately gone to his aid, instead of becoming bitter toward him ignorantly taking everything personally allowing a 'root of bitterness' to rise up in my heart against the very man God had sent me to serve and help. Finally, on one Sunday night in the middle of the service, unprovoked the pastor's wife stood up and yelled, 'I don't want to go to the mission field.' Nothing had ever been said about them going to the mission field, but there she was defiantly shouting to God and everyone else that she refused to leave her family and do what everyone knew God had called them to do. It was common knowledge the pastor's greatest joy in the ministry was his heart for the mission fields of the world. It's all he ever talked about.

Consequently, he allowed both Vietnamese and Korean congregations to use our building as a worship center. His greatest desire was to one day actually be on the mission field rather than in the pulpit of a church in Florida. That Sunday night his wife spoke those deadly words I watched him die to a lifelong dream. It was in that instant I realized how terribly I had missed God in my relationship with this broken, weary man. From that day onward my attitude and life radically changed as I learned a great lesson. I had been 'the guy' the Lord led into the midst of the bitter waters of that precious man's life. Instead of seeing the hand of the Lord in the whole process, I only saw the flaws in the man. By His grace I will never make that mistake again. In the months following that Sunday night service our relationship took a God size turn and we became friends and even comrades in the ministry. Not surprisingly, it wasn't long after that the Lord released me to move on in the ministry. I was then led by the Holy Spirit to Indiana to work side by side with a pastor who continually honored and supported all the Lord had called me to do. It was under this man's leadership the ministry of Harvest was birthed. That man's name is Pastor Dave Faris, a gentle, but mighty man of God.

Remembering these stories from the past helps us maintain our focus in the present. Even though we are presently in the midst of some bitter waters, we are confident our steps have been ordered by the Lord and He is in the midst of this momentary bitterness. We are also confident He will perform the impossible and turn our bitter pool (circumstances) into pure, sweet water. Thank You, Lord!

Prayer

Dear Lord,

Help me to find the place of praise in the midst of these bitter waters that have overwhelmed the banks of my stability and peace. Forgive my unbelieving, anxious and grumbling heart. Open the eyes of my heart that I may confidently know what is the hope of Your calling in my life. If possible, and I know nothing is impossible with You, please turn the bitter waters that have invaded my life into a place of sweetness in Your presence. Should the bitterness tarry, give me the courage to stand with a steadfast assurance the days ahead will be better than all the days behind. Help me in this moment to trust Your Word which says You will not allow anything more than I can endure to come my way, but with the temptation will always provide a Way of escape. Help me confidently rest in the knowledge that You would never have led me this way at this time for my destruction, but have done so for my good and Your glory. I know You are with me in this place of uncertainty and difficulty. Thank You for Your promise to never leave or forsake me. I know that with You by my side no weapon formed against me can prosper. Thank You, Lord. Amen.

A mighty fortress is our God, a bulwark never failing
Our Helper, He amid the flood of mortal ills prevailing
For still our ancient foe doth seek to work us woe
His craft and power are great, and armed with cruel hate
On earth is not his equal.

And though this world with devils filled should threaten to undo us
We will not fear for God hath willed
His truth to triumph through us
The prince of darkness grim, we tremble not for him
His rage we can endure for lo his doom is sure
One little word shall fell him.

God is faithful, Who will not allow you to be tempted beyond what you are able, but with the temptation will also make the way of escape, that you may be able to bear it. 1 Corinthians 10:13

The Story Behind the Song:

We can all identify with those seasons in our lives wherein we spend more energy whining than we do worshipping the Lord. This most commonly occurs when circumstances abruptly change or things don't go the way we had envisioned them going. That's when anxiety and pressure begins to build in our thoughts which opens the floodgates for stress to take hold. Stress is a direct product of worrying, and worrying in the life of a believer is a sin. It was the mid 1990's and I was being stretched tighter than a kite string in a hurricane. We had already invested tens of thousands of dollars and nearly two months of tireless work into recording the *Carry On* project, but something still wasn't right. I still needed that 'one' song to tie the project together, but after going through nearly sixty song ideas I still didn't have that last song I knew I needed to complete the project.

By this time we were all physically and mentally exhausted working well past midnight every night. Consequently, we decided to set aside the next few mornings to get some much needed rest. On one of those mornings, while everyone was still in a dead sleep, the Lord awakened me. I quickly arose and made my way to my quiet place where I spent my personal time with the Lord. Almost instantly His presence filled the room and all the stress and worry left. Then the Lord began to remind me of my own personal journey over the past several years, a journey that had been laden with countless attacks, betrayals, pitfalls, failures and disappointments, and how through it all He had faithfully brought me through safe and sound. In that moment I was ashamed and repented of my worrying, then turned my heart to worship and praise Him for His patience, mercy, kindness and faithfulness. As I began to sing a new song to Him and worship Him Who is worthy of all praise, He birthed within my spirit the chords and lyrics to *Highway to Holiness.* This new song unto the Lord flowed out effortlessly until it was a finished product, the 'right' song to finish the *Carry On* project. Later that afternoon I introduced *Highway to Holiness* for the first time to the guys in the studio and it became the missing link to the entire project. To God be all the glory.

Highway to Holiness

(A song from the "Carry On" project, music and lyrics written by Jerry Williams)

When the raging storms of this life draw near...
Your faith seems far away
He will lead you on from the times of fear
Through His love and faithfulness.

Through the years of life, all the memories held...
The times of joy and pain
You can see beyond the darkened veil
A road that leads to Him.

Chorus:
Though the highway of holiness
May be lined with tears and pain.
Still it leads on to righteousness
For the faithful One who stands.

Through the failures we have all endured,
The triumphs that they bring
There's a light beyond our deepest wound
That always leads to Him.

Though the highway of holiness
May be lined with tears and pain.
Still it leads on to righteousness
For the faithful One who stands.

These things I have spoken to you, that in Me you may have peace. In the world you will have tribulation, but be of good cheer, I have overcome the world.
John 16:33

DAY 5 MORE BLESSED TO GIVE

And as you go, preach, saying, 'The kingdom of heaven is at hand.' Heal the sick, cleanse the lepers, raise the dead, cast out demons. Freely you have received, freely give. Matthew 10:7-8 NKJV

In 1999 and 2000 I had a young man, Brandon, who worked in our home studio with me. He was a long-haired, fun and very talented young man, but like most guys twenty years of age he would do just about 'anything' on a dare or whim. One little tidbit I quickly learned about him was he would go to almost any lengths to acquire just about anything that was being advertised as 'free'. In his twenty-year-old way of thinking anything being offered for 'free' simply couldn't be passed up, no matter what it was. For example, for a limited time only a local sandwich shop launched a promotion stating that anyone bald coming in on Monday's would receive a 'free' sub sandwich. The promotional was called 'Bald Monday's'. You guessed it, without hesitation Brandon shaved his head down to the skin just to get his 'free' sub sandwich the next Monday. Most of us aren't that crazy or impulsive, but oh how we all love wearing, eating or using those gifts that are freely given to us during birthdays, Christmas, anniversaries, etc. Some of those 'free' gifts become so special to us they remain with us for many years afterwards, such as the Gibson CL50 guitar my mother 'freely' gave me in 1999 when we first launched EPIC Ministries. All these years later it is still my most cherished guitar, even though I obviously didn't pay for it. We all have 'free gifts' such as my guitar that we have openly embraced without any thought or concerns of their ownership.

They are "free gifts" given out of love, commitment and friendship.

Consider for a moment God's indescribable 'free Gift' offered to every human being: For God so loved the world (you) He GAVE His only begotten Son. God has given the Greatest and most valuable Gift of all, His only Son, Jesus, as a "free Gift" of Salvation to all who willingly receive Him. Yes, this indescribable Gift is free, but do not misunderstand that it carries with it eternally binding responsibilities and unalterable conditions. What exactly does that mean? It's much like the time I purchased my oldest daughter's first vehicle in 1991. She had passed Driver's Education and had received her driver's license, but had no possible way of acquiring her own vehicle, paying the insurance, keeping it full of fuel, maintaining the oil and filters, etc. Because I loved her and had committed ALL my resources to her as my daughter, out of my personal resources I purchased, the vehicle I joyfully and 'freely' offered to her as a token of my love and commitment to her. She was extremely grateful, but clearly understood such a costly gift carried with it responsibilities and requirements that had to be kept if she wanted to continue freely using her 'free gift'. For her own protection I made it clear that until she proved she could (and would) ABIDE by the laws that are in place to protect every driver on the road, she would not be allowed to drive her 'free gift' on the highways. She willingly took ownership and full responsibility for her 'free' gift which made her daddy really proud.

In much the same way the 'free' Gift of Salvation through Jesus is offered to everyone in the world. It is an extremely costly 'GIFT' and nothing to ever be trifled with or approached irresponsibly. What a priceless Gift we have been given in Christ. All the benefits, blessings, attributes and privileges Jesus possesses as both God and man have been freely bestowed upon us. What an amazing GIFT! What an amazing responsibility that our heavenly Father would entrust to us to share with all the world. I'm not really sure any one of us can fully grasp the enormity of so great a 'free' gift.

Before we go any further I must ask: Are you confident you are truly born again and without any doubt are a child of God? If you can't answer 'yes' to that question, then pause and call out to Jesus right now. The 'free GIFT' of Salvation is waiting to be opened. All He requires is that you come humbly before Him, turn from your rebellious way of living and call upon Him for mercy and forgiveness acknowledging your need for Him to be your Savior. His promise is, 'Whoever calls upon the name of the Lord will be saved' (Acts 2:21). Salvation is FREE, but cannot be acquired any other way. Jesus is the only Door, the only Way! You have to accept this indescribable 'free gift' on His terms. If you are willing and repentant, then you will immediately receive the 'Free Gift' of eternal salvation, and be forever grafted into the family of God. Hallelujah!

For those who have by grace through faith already received this indescribable GIFT, the great news is that Salvation isn't a 'one and done' Gift, like the chocolate pecan turtles I so loved getting last year. Jesus continues to 'save' throughout the extent of our days. This is great news because we all periodically fall back into old rebellious habits thereby breaking our commitment to keep the requirements that came with the 'free gift'. When we do that while driving we get pulled over and issued a ticket for breaking the law. It's no different with our heavenly Father. When we abuse His INDESCRIBABLE GIFT and find ourselves once again prisoner to some lingering sin or memory of past failure, then the Holy Spirit pulls us over and gives us a ticket reminding us of our responsibility to honor the FREE GIFT. If we continue to disobey, then we become impounded until we repent. Are you presently impounded? If so, then immediately stop what you are doing and take a look inside the closets of your heart and soul! There among all your other forgotten and unused free gifts and possessions is "Freedom". This is one of the measureless benefits you freely received when you accepted God's greatest Gift, Jesus! If you will cry out to your heavenly Father just as you did when you first accepted His 'free gift', then He will immediately reinstate all your heavenly privileges and set you FREE! Are you weak and under attack from the enemy of your soul? Then reach back into your closet and embrace His "power" which overcomes all the power and schemes of the enemy. In that moment you will realize His promise really is true that no weapon formed against you will prosper (Isaiah 54:17). Remember, His power is already yours in and through the "Free Gift" you've been given. Are you lonely, sick, diseased, broken or spiritually dry and destitute? Then open your eyes and see the boundless treasure chest you already have in Jesus! It's right in front of you! Through Him you have been given everything you need for life and godliness (2 Peter 1:3). All the fullness of the Godhead dwells within Him Who now lives within your heart. He is in you as your covenant possession from God the Father! All other gifts pale in comparison to the greatest "Gift" of all, Jesus!

In August of 1990, while performing a concert in Alexandria, Louisiana, I had an amazing encounter with the Lord over this very subject. I had been spending more time than usual pondering 'Who' this Jesus really IS and ALL He has brought with Him to fulfill His purpose and calling in and through my life. During the week leading up to the concert in Alexandria I had been overwhelmed with a spirit of thankfulness to our heavenly Father for the indescribable 'Gift' of His Son. During the concert the next week something completely unexpected happened while I was on stage. I was in the middle of performing a song to a packed auditorium when suddenly the Lord invaded my thoughts asking me a single question. How I made it through the remainder of the song is not certain, but the direction of the concert was radically altered as a result of this unexpected question. Just prior to the 'question' I had glanced at my twelve-year-old son who was standing just off stage behind the curtains. It was an extremely rare opportunity for him to be with me, but since Alexandria wasn't too far from our ministry headquarters in East Texas I was able to have him with me on the trip. Only moments after glancing at my son the Lord asked me this question: If I promised you that every single person in this auditorium would be eternally saved if you willingly give your son's life for their salvation, would you give up his life for theirs? I was instantaneously overwhelmed with emotion as I began to consider the COST of giving up my ONLY son for someone else's life. As soon as the song was finished I stood staring at the capacity crowd and began to weep. No one knew what was taking place as I stood there weeping. Then I called for my son to come and stand next to me on the stage. I then began to relate to the packed auditorium what the Lord had just asked me, all the while embracing my son holding him in a loving, but protective manner. I finally broke and proclaimed to everyone in the auditorium as well as to the Lord, 'No, I'm not willing to give my son's life for these I don't even know'. I went on to say I was more than willing to give my own life for them, but did not have the depth of love or compassion to offer my ONLY son's life in their place. A silence fell over the crowd as the Lord began to powerfully move through each heart present. Within moments people began rising and coming to the front of the auditorium crying out to the Lord for mercy, forgiveness and salvation. That night blinded eyes were opened to see the incredible 'Free Gift' given to them from the Father in heaven. At that point I grabbed my guitar and sang:

Jesus loves you, this I know, for the Bible tells me so
Little ones to Him belong, they are weak, but He is strong!

Yes, Jesus loves you! Yes, Jesus loves you!
Yes, Jesus loves you! The Bible tells me so!

As His children we all make up the extended "Body of Christ" in the world. Therefore, as His Body we are now His designed and chosen extension of this indescribable "Free Gift" to the world. As we go forth throughout this year, may His love, power, grace, mercy, forgiveness, holiness, righteousness, deliverance, freedom and living Word be freely offered in and through each of our lives. Freely you have received! Freely give!

I am the LORD, I have called you in righteousness, I will also hold you by the hand and watch over you, and I will appoint you as a covenant to the people, as a light to the nations, to open blind eyes, to bring out prisoners from the dungeon, and those who dwell in darkness from the prison. Isaiah 42:6-7

But you are a chosen race, a royal priesthood, a holy nation, a people for God's own possession, that you may proclaim the excellencies of Him who has called you out of darkness into His marvelous light; for you once were not a people, but now you are the people of God; you had not received mercy, but now you have received mercy. 1 Peter 2:9-10

Prayer

Dear Father, thank You for loving me while I was yet a sinner, and in every aspect wholly unlovable. Thank You for sending Your only Son, Jesus, to be Your Free Gift of Life, Hope, freedom and deliverance for me. Forgive me for too often being more focused on me rather than You and all You have freely provided for me through Jesus. Help me in the days to come to live in such a way that others might see You in me and thus ask how they might receive such a wonderful free Gift. Set a guard over my heart that my desire for 'things' would decrease as my desire for You increases. Teach me all Your ways that I might be fully pleasing to You. I love You, Lord, and truly thank You for this indescribable free Gift of Life.

Whom have I in heaven but You. And on earth I desire nothing but You. My flesh and my heart may fail, but You are the strength of my heart and my portion forever. Amen. Psalm 73:25

I hear the Savior say,
'Thy strength indeed is small'
'Child of weakness watch and pray
Find in Me thine all in all

Jesus paid it all! All to Him I owe!
Sin had left a crimson stain. He washed it white as snow!

For nothing good have I
Whereby Thy grace to claim
I'll wash my garments white
In the blood of Calvary's Lamb

Jesus paid it all! All to Him I owe!
Sin had left a crimson stain. He washed it white as snow!

The Story Behind the Song:

As a musician, songwriter and singer I've always longed to write and one day produce a Christmas music project containing all original music. Although that desire has never fully materialized, I have written and recorded several songs specifically for the message of Christmas. One of those songs is The Gift. This song was miraculously birthed out of the ashes of another very difficult year that had left me reeling as a father trying to cope with the multitude of mistakes I seemingly continued to make in my attempts to maintain peace and stability in our home. Feeling overwhelmed by my own inconsistencies and inadequacies as a parent, I decided to pour myself into decorating our entire ministry campus for Christmas. As I began the process (which took several days) a wonderfully strange thing began to happen. The more I focused on decorating the property for Christmas, the more I became focused on the reason for the season. By the end of the week I was no longer dominated and stressed about the mountain of trouble in my home, but was instead consumed with celebrating the amazing Gift of God's Love in Christ. This spilled over into a musical expression of worship which inspired me to write this simple, but wonderful song.

The Gift

(A song from the "41 Will Come" project, music and lyrics written by Jerry Williams)

A star is shining out tonight leading with its holy light
Onward to the place where Life begins
Saying with each ray of Hope that on this night a Child is born
And one day He will reign as King of kings.

The angels in the heavens shout, "Glory!" to this holy Child
All the creatures of the earth give praise!
Let every man rejoice and sing for God has chosen now to bring
The Gift of His Own Son to us today.

Even as a Child He knows one day soon His earthly throne
Will be a tree of shame on which to die
But still in love He chose to come, the Lamb of God, His only Son
Pouring out His love for all mankind.

The angels in the heavens shout, "Glory!" to this holy Child
All the creatures of the earth give praise!
Let every man rejoice and sing for God has chosen now to bring
The Gift of His Own Son to us today.

DAY 6 PREOCCUPIED WITH CHRIST

As the deer pants for the water brooks, so my soul pants for You, O God. My soul thirsts for God, for the living God. Psalm 42:1, 2

The late A. W. Tozer said in one of his books, *We are called to an everlasting preoccupation with God*. Wow! Do you really believe this? 'Preoccupation' means to be in a state in which you give ALL your attention to something. If what Tozer says is true, and I am certain it is, then one can't help but wonder if the majority of those who profess to be the true children of God in the earth have completely overlooked and missed this all important issue. How often do you meet people, even those in the ministry, who you would be compelled to say are completely 'preoccupied' in their hearts and minds with Christ? I know how difficult that can be, especially in the fast paced world in which we live today. Even within the confines of our own home we have to continually ask the Lord to permeate and consume our hearts afresh with an insatiable desire, love and occupation for Him alone. How easily and quickly we become ignorantly preoccupied with lesser pursuits that slowly diminish our desire to continuously and passionately pursue our mighty God. I can still hear the faint sounds of the old saints singing:

Spirit of the living God fall afresh on me!
Spirit of the living God fall afresh on me!
Melt me, mold me, make me, use me!
Spirit of the living God fall afresh on me!

One of the biggest pitfalls I have personally wrestled with throughout all my years in the ministry is getting caught up in pursuing the 'benefits' of God rather than simply pursuing Him. We are clearly instructed in His word to *forget none of His benefits* (Psalm 103:2), but far too often we become so focused and preoccupied with pursuing these heavenly "benefits" (which are freely ours in Christ) that we become distracted and lose sight of the main thing which is knowing Christ. Consequently, we eventually overlook our need to first pursue and bless the One Who has lovingly provided these benefits for us. For this reason, I don't believe it would be an overstatement to say the Church today is filled with millions who have unknowingly and carelessly become pursuers of God's "things" rather than pursuers of God Himself.

The essence of our lives as believers is simply to KNOW Him and be KNOWN by Him. There is a conscious intimacy that's available between God and His children that cannot exist in any other religion the world has to offer. How magnificent and marvelous to be pursued and intimately known by the God Who created the universe. That is the marvel and the mystery of the love of God available to every man, woman and child through the Life, Name and Blood of the incarnate Christ. No wonder the angels sing, *Worthy is the Lamb Who was slain*!

Thankfully, I have learned to regularly take time to review the inventory of those "things" which occupy my life. When was the last time you asked yourself the following questions:

- Where is the majority of my leisure time spent?
- What are the things that dominate most of my time, energy and thoughts?
- What is the primary focus of my desires for the future?

These are the questions I have often asked myself through the years. More often than not each time I revisit these questions personally the Lord usually reveals some area in my life that's out of balance and needs immediate adjusting. The marvelous 'gifts' God graciously and freely gives to each of us who KNOW Him were NEVER designed to be the *objects* of our faith, hope and love. On the contrary, He alone MUST be the Objective of our faith, the Object of our hope, and the Object of our love. After all, He alone is the Source of everything we need for life and godliness.

Whom have I in heaven but You? And besides You, I desire nothing on earth. My flesh and my heart may fail, but God is the strength of my heart and my portion forever. Psalm 73:25,26

I am truly grateful God is so loving and patient with me. Each time I stray He gently leads me back to that secret place wherein He is once again the preeminent occupation of my heart. He is all that is truly necessary or needed in my life. He is the Way, the Truth, and the Life. In Him alone are found the riches of grace, mercy and forgiveness. Therefore, anything that precedes my singular pursuit of Him wrongly becomes the preoccupation of my spirit, soul and mind, and therein is destined to become a stumbling block to His presence manifesting in my heart and life.

You're all I want! You're all I've ever needed!
You're all I want! Help me know You are here!

As a songwriter I fully understand that it's common practice to sing songs in our services without any real knowledge of the possible bitter struggle that took place in the heart and spirit of the one who wrote the song. As a Psalmist I often muse about the circumstances that led the writer to pen the words we are presently singing. That's why I can easily identify with the writer of the above lyrics. I know all too well the unending wrestling match between spirit and soul when trying to find God in the midst of so much daily confusion, activity and responsibility. That's why I continually renew my vow to be completely preoccupied with our awesome God and to seek Him first in every situation and circumstance. Oh, may we all become fully convinced that any casual approach to this holy business will allow our deceitful hearts to conquer in the end. As for me and my house we refuse to pamper our feelings or move slowly forward in this 'preoccupation' with God. We MUST have God Himself at all costs! Nothing else and none other will satisfy! We are fully aware that within each of us is an ancient curse that instinctively causes us to be possessive and crave "things". However, we are determined to never, never, never give in to the cravings of our decaying flesh! Instead, we choose to willingly walk the highway of renunciation that God might be the sole preoccupation of our hearts and reign supremely over every detail of our lives.

What, or who is it that preoccupies your heart and mind right now? Are you afraid of losing some *thing* or *someone*? Remember, Jesus didn't come to destroy, but to save. Cast yourself defenseless before His presence and take hold of the horns of the altar. Without hesitation let Him rip out by the very roots any *thing* other than Him that has preoccupied your heart and mind. If you willingly do this the chasm between you and His manifest presence will be instantly removed and you will be flooded with the river of His delights. If you willingly allow Him to do this without defending yourself in any way, the end result will be a life identified by His presence, power, anointing and blessings.

A man's life consists not in the abundance of the things which he possesses. Luke 12:15

God impoverishes only to make rich, becoming in secret Himself the Substitute for all that He takes away from the soul. Jeanne Guyon

Idolatry is not only the adoration of images, but also trust in one's own righteousness, works and merits, and putting confidence in riches and power. Martin Luther

Prayer

Dear Father,

I acknowledge there are 'things' keeping me continually distracted from placing my life completely in Your charge and control. I long for You to once again be the sole preoccupation and domination of the desires of my heart. I fully acknowledge my tendencies toward being slothful in my pursuit of You and Your presence without which I am helpless and blind. Cause my heart to seek, love and desire only You. Upon faith in Your Word I now boldly draw near to You for help and assurance. Thank You for being here with me. Consecrate my heart and mind so that in the days to come present distractions will be nothing more than a remembrance of things past.

Take my life and let it be consecrated Lord, to Thee
Take my hands and let them move at the impulse of Thy love
Take my feet and let them be swift and beautiful for Thee
Take my voice and let me sing always only for my King
Take my silver and my gold not a mite would I withhold
Take my moments and my days let them flow in ceaseless praise
Take my will and make it Thine it shall be no longer mine
Take my heart, it is Thine Own, it shall be Thy royal throne. Amen.

The Story Behind the Song:

Besides You, I desire nothing on earth. That was the eventual cry of Asaph's heart in Psalm 73, but not until he had wrestled with his own negative and pitiful thoughts that were screaming in his head telling him the wicked were better off in the land than the righteous. Much like Asaph, in 2007 I had fallen into a similar pity party and attitude of negativity completely preoccupied with the circumstances rather than preoccupied with the promises of my faithful God. At the time we were living full time on a 40-foot motor coach traveling around the nation ministering to ministers who were in need of encouragement and personal support. Our time on the coach lasted a little more than five years, but it wasn't all glorious or glamourous. Surprisingly there were many weeks of isolation and loneliness spent hanging out in Wal-Mart parking lots wondering where next to go. During one of those lonely 'down' times when no one was reaching out to us and the phones were deadly silent, I became preoccupied with the following thoughts, 'Is this all there is? What's the use in continuing to try and live this life? It's too hard, costs too much and takes far too long before you see any tangible evidence that what we're doing is actually making a difference in anyone's life.' Early one morning as I was wallowing in my self-pity the Lord crashed in on my pity party and spoke these words to my heart, 'My son, do not be afraid!' It was then I realized I was actually gripped with worry and fear concerning the future. In that moment I did what Asaph did, I made my way to0 the sanctuary of God. Instantly the mental fog lifted and I clearly discerned where I was, what I was doing and who was behind all the negativity. I cried out to the Lord repenting of my unbelief and proceeded to write *A Consecrated Life* as an offering of praise to the Lord.

A Consecrated Life

(Song on the Gideon project, music and lyrics written by Jerry Williams)

You've heard my voice, You've heard my cry
You said, 'My son do not fear'.
You promised, then You redeemed my life
And Lord that's why I'm here

You said if I'd draw near to You
Then You'd draw near to me
So Lord I've come, but still the wonder
Is You've come to me

Chorus
So once again upon this altar Lord I lay my life
Take it and now Lord, forever
Let it glorify, only You, only You

Lord, help me to see what You see in me
Teach me how to stand
So often my thoughts only see my faults
When You see a mighty man

You know my sin, You know my shame
But still You died for me
How can it be You took my place
And chose to set me free

Look, as the clay is in the Potter's hand,
so are you in My hand!
Jeremiah 18:5-6

DAY 7 IN THE WORKSHOP OF GOD

For a righteous man may fall seven times and rise again, but the wicked shall fall by calamity. Proverbs 24:16

Several years ago while doing a concert in Nashville, Tennessee, my 1980 Martin D-28 acoustic guitar was accidentally knocked over on stage. As I rapidly made my way over to what was far and away my favorite guitar I immediately knew something was terribly wrong. As I picked up the old guitar I saw the undeniable proof of what I feared had happened. As a result of the fall, my old guitar had suffered a complete break across the area where the tuning keys are located and the majority of the tension from the strings exists. Although still attached, the strings were now flopping loosely against the fret board and the once beautiful sounding instrument was rendered completely unplayable. Following the concert, the immediate diagnosis from those who looked at the broken instrument (this was the guitar I did the majority of my songwriting with) was that it was hopelessly damaged and regrettably beyond repair. Most of us felt there was nothing left to do but throw the instrument away or use it for parts. Ken Pennel, the Director of A & R for the Benson Company (my record label at the time), asked me if I would mind if he sent it back to the factory where it was originally created. I thanked him for his concern for the instrument and his kind offer, then with little confidence let him take the old guitar with him. It remained at the Martin factory so long I slowly began losing any hope of it ever being repaired. Eventually, after more than six months without any word concerning the old guitar, I completely forgot about the instrument and moved on with several other guitars, none of which had the same feeling or sound as my old D-28. Then the unexpected happened. After nearly eight months I was surprisingly contacted by the Martin factory with a simple alert that the instrument was finally being returned. Nothing else was stated in the memo. When the glorious day finally came and it arrived by UPS I couldn't wait to open the case and play the old guitar again. Inside the case a note was attached expressing regret for the length of time it had taken for the repairs, but then expressing how an unusually natural bond had been achieved in the area that had been broken leaving the once damaged crown now stronger than the original wood. Hallelujah! After months of painstakingly slow restorative work this same instrument, the very guitar that had previously been proclaimed unusable and forever lost, was now actually better and stronger than when it was first created. The impossible became reality!

Since that time, I have joyfully used that same old guitar, the one everyone had labeled 'worthless', to write and record hundreds of songs. I have also taken it with me around the world ministering along the way to thousands of people. Its restored ability to do what it was created to do, make beautiful music, has now touched the hearts and lives of millions of people to the glory of our awesome God.

As I was recently changing the strings on this old guitar the Lord spoke to my heart and said:

Son, as your Creator I am doing to the broken areas of your heart what was done to your old guitar. You and many others thought the instrument of your life was ruined forever, but I am making the bond between you and Me even stronger than before. Just as the music from that old guitar has gotten sweeter and purer with age, so will the music of your life be for Me in the days to come.

What an incredible promise! What an infusion of Hope for the days to come! But wait! Remember that God is no respecter of persons and has no favorites among all His children. He loves us all equally. If He will do this wonderful work of restoration for me, then He will certainly do it for you. Therefore, instead of looking at the broken pieces of your past, make the decision right now to willingly allow your Creator to take you aside in His workshop for as long as He deems necessary to completely restore your broken areas. Even if it takes longer than you would expect, it will result in the sweetest music ever heard coming forth from the instrument of your life.

For I know the plans that I have for you, declares the LORD, plans for welfare and not for calamity to give you a future and a hope. Jeremiah 29:11

I have often shared this story of my old Martin guitar when building new relationships with leaders around the nation. Initially with each new relationship I find it's very common for leaders to take the first available opportunity to bring up any seasons of failure in their past. With many of these precious individuals I quickly discover they've given up hope of ever truly fulfilling God's destiny in their lives. Try and imagine what it must be like being committed to doing something with your life that you have no real confidence can ever be fully accomplished. It would be like trying to play that old Martin guitar without having it actually fixed. I could have easily taken matters into my own hands and in haste glued the broken crown. After all it was my guitar and I know enough to at least try something to help make it better. The reason I didn't even consider trying was I knew I didn't have the tools or ability to successfully undertake such a task. Therefore, without any hope of success, I had no confidence to even begin.

With more than 20,000 ordained ministers leaving the ministry each year in the West it's easy to see that thousands of these precious leaders are living without hope for their future. It doesn't take a Nobel Prize winner to discern the deadly schemes of the enemy in this mass exodus of leaders from the Church. Just last night I had the honor of praying and counseling with a sixty-eight-year-old brother who had once again been taken captive by the memories of his past rebellion, sin and failure. This brother is full of the Word of God, yet in an instant was broken (just like my old guitar) and deemed unusable. Praise the Lord! All I did with this precious brother last night was send him back to the workshop of His Creator, and that's where he still remains today. It's amazing how spending a little time under repair in the workshop of God's magnificent presence has the power to fully restore our broken lives, and set us completely free from the strongholds of the past while renewing our hope for the future.

You will show me the path of life. In Your presence is fullness of joy. At Your right hand are pleasures forevermore. Psalms 16:11

If we walk in the light as He Himself is in the light, we have fellowship with one another, and the blood of Jesus His Son cleanses us from all sin. 1 John 1:7

Jesus proclaimed, *These things I have spoken to you, that in Me you may have peace. In the world you have tribulation, but take courage, I have overcome the world.* John 16:33

Eventually everyone will experience seasons of trouble, tribulation and even momentary tragedy. Many will even suffer being broken while doing the very thing they were created and destined to do for God. When those seasons occur do not be surprised when untested, untried men quickly line up and proclaim you are finished, unusable and unable to ever be fixed. However, in the midst of your brokenness there will always be someone ready to send you back to your Creator. Time in the factory will prove the unexpected devastating break will only lead to your becoming stronger in the days to come. The Creator isn't looking at your broken state with disdain and displeasure, but instead His gaze is one of pure love and perfect understanding. We are His workmanship created in Christ Jesus and all carry His DNA in our lives. He knows we are weak, and has made every provision to extend His strength, power, sustenance and healing to us if we will confidently trust and rely on Him to 'fix' the broken areas of the instrument of our lives.

I charge each of you to make the decision to cease gazing upon the broken crowns of all your past disappointments, failures, broken relationships and sins. He saw them before He ever created and chose you. Ask, and then trust Him to open the eyes of your heart that you may once again behold Him Who holds you firmly in His hands and has promised to never leave or forsake you. Make haste and run to Him Who dwells in the evergreen high places where there is an endless supply of everything we need to bear the tension of life and ministry. Can you hear Him beckoning even now as you read this?

Come to Me, all who are weary and heavy-laden, and I will give you rest. Take My yoke upon you, and learn from Me, for I am gentle and humble in heart, and you shall find rest for your souls. For My yoke is easy, and My burden is light. Matthew 11:28-30

Prayer

Dear Father,

When I am broken and beyond finding help apart from Your loving, caring touch, grant me the precious gift of hearing Your voice assuring me that by the stripes of Your Son I truly am healed. I am so easily discouraged by flagrant character flaws that continually proclaim me guilty. Yet, in Your bosom I have found pardon and future purpose. Enlarge my faith and renew my confidence that You have truly destined me to become that which is pleasing in Your sight. Thank You for Your amazing patience and care with me. Thank You for not disqualifying me for the flaws that still exist in my heart or the wrongs I have committed along the way. Thank You for favoring, forgiving and blessing me with the bounty of heaven, instead of giving me what I deserve. Thank You for promising You will actually complete the work You've begun in me. Thank You for establishing plans for me that are not for calamity, but for my welfare and Your praise in the earth. Should there still be cracks in my heart and mind that are yet unhealed, I ask You to quickly heal and seal them in the mercy and grace that surrounds Your throne. I love You above all else and thank You for restoring me to a place of victory and effective use in Your hands. Amen.

<u>The Story Behind the Song:</u>

It had been just a few weeks after I was radically born again that I was invited to go visit a young teenage girl who needed Jesus in her life. Denny Vaughn, the young man who had led me to Christ, was taking me to meet her. I was thrilled to get another opportunity to speak with someone about my new life in Christ, but when we drove into the parking lot I became immediately confused. Denny hadn't said much on our way to meet this young girl, but now that we were pulling up to the front entrance of a funeral home a sick feeling began to grip my heart. As we stepped inside he quietly led me to a room toward the back of the building. The room was completely empty except for a casket at the far end. He then asked me to go and look in the open casket. When I reached the casket lying inside was the lifeless body of a beautiful teenage girl who had somehow lost all hope for the future and taken her own life. In that moment something rose up in my spirit and I cried out to the Lord asking Him to anoint me with the power to see these hopeless souls delivered and saved. God answered that prayer that day, and over the years I have been honored to see the Lord touch, change, deliver and redeem thousands of lives, many of which were these broken, hopeless lives who were literally on the precipice of disaster and death. There's really no way to recall how many times I've encountered individuals who had lost all hope and had become suicidal. In each of those instances God has consistently anointed me to be His messenger speaking His words of Hope into what appeared to be a hopeless situation. The following song *Carry On* was birthed out of many of these encounters with hopeless and broken individuals who miraculously found Jesus to be their HEALER and their blessed HOPE. To God be all the glory! Amen and Amen!

Carry On
(A song from the "Carry On" project, written by Jerry Williams)

In the darkened corners of your quiet hiding place
In the shadows of your secret lonely world
There you dream of perfect Love you hunger to embrace
All your fantasies, your visions and your hopes

Let Me heal your wounded heart, let Me open up your eyes
Let Me show you all the love I long to give to you tonight
Let Me give you courage and the strength to carry on...I Am the Lord!

When your dreams have faded and your heart is giving in
To the pressure of the forces in control
And when you feel you've missed the only chance you had to win
You long to leave the only world you know

Let Me heal your wounded heart, let Me open up your eyes
Let Me show you all the love I long to give to you tonight
Let Me give you courage and the strength to carry on...I Am the Lord!

Repair us, O God Almighty!
Make Your face shine upon us,
that we may be saved. Psalms 80:7

DAY 8 TROUBLE IN THE CAMP

...and when they had come to Mysia they were trying to go into Bithynia, and the Spirit of Jesus did not permit them. Acts 16:7

Throughout all the years I attended Jr. and Sr. High School I was involved with athletics starting in several sports. Basketball was my favorite sport to play, but my lack of physical size greatly limited my ability to excel in the sport the older I became. For example, throughout all those years playing basketball there was one specific goal I attempted over and over to accomplish, but never was able to achieve. What was it? Being able to physically jump high enough to touch the rim. It was so easy for others I eventually became consumed with a desire to one day be the little white guy who could jump high enough to touch the rim. Year after year I continuously worked out focusing on building up the necessary leg strength to jump high enough to touch the elusive rim others touched so easily. No matter how hard I tried or trained I never achieved the unreachable goal because the Lord didn't create me with the necessary physical attributes to fulfill the long sought after desire.

In the opening verse (Acts 16:7) the word "trying" means, *to test or prove by trial through discipline.* I can certainly relate to all the Apostle Paul and *some of the leading men among the brethren* (Acts 15:22) 'tried' to do for the Lord. They didn't just sit around and discuss the potential or possibility of traveling to Bithynia. On the contrary, they corporately endeavored to go, and then followed through with weeks of prayer and serious preparation to eventually enter that country. However, all their personal endeavors ended up being for naught as they eventually realized the Lord was not at this time commissioning them to go into Bithynia. Therefore, they regrettably abandoned their plans and moved forward in a different direction with their journey.

I have been in exactly this same place in the ministry many times over the years. There has to be at least a dozen times I have received a specific 'word' from the Lord, then zealously committed myself to seeing that 'word' accomplished, only to then have the Holy Spirit tell me after I had expended great amounts of time, energy, prayer and finances, it wasn't the right time. This can be very frustrating and confusing for anyone who is genuinely seeking to 'do' ALL the Lord is calling them to 'do' for His glory. Had Paul and the others lost their ability to hear the voice of God? Was there insincerity somewhere in their desire to go into Bithynia? Did God secretly change His plans for them just to see how they would react? The answer to all of these questions is emphatically "NO"! Of course they still knew how to listen for and hear the voice of God. Without question they were diligently seeking Him in prayer and the Word. The idea God would ever toy with His children or play cruel mind games with them is absurd and ignorant, and directly in contrast to His nature and character. Still, the facts remain hidden concerning why the Lord didn't allow them to go into Bithynia.

As a pastor and ministry leader I am fully aware how sudden changes in already agreed upon plans can affect the morale of the whole congregation or leadership team. Not every team member embraces sudden change easily. As I pondered this real life situation that occurred in Paul's ministry team I couldn't help but wonder about the potentially negative ramifications that might have resonated throughout the other members of the team when Paul's initial decision to go to Bithynia was abandoned. If you've ever been through a situation like this, you can well imagine some of the unsettling comments that could have easily been buzzing throughout the camp. Whenever team members begin murmuring it almost always leads to confusion which is never a good thing. When left unchecked, murmuring evolves into grumbling which gives way to dissension within the team. Can you envision how the Pharisees who followed Paul day and night might have quickly seized the moment taking this opportunity to challenge the validity of Paul's calling and office? Can you hear them questioning his character and commitment while mocking the team members who had left their families and businesses to go on this journey with him? After all, the team didn't exactly begin the trip with a united spirit of joy and expectation. On the contrary, just prior to leaving there arose a strong disagreement between Paul and Barnabas over John Mark's commitment, which resulted in Barnabas and John Mark leaving the team. Now can you see the potential powder keg that might have easily been existing in Paul's team? How was Paul going to handle this now? What was he going to do? Simple: Re-focus, obey God and finish the journey!

This account in Paul's life reminds me of a time in 1975 when I was on my first overseas mission trip to Korea. There was a powerful anointing on the team that had been assembled which resulted in thousands of souls being saved, demons being cast out and many being healed. Just before heading back home, a group of godly men who were recognized as key leaders of the Korean Church graciously asked if I would pray about staying in their country and devoting the rest of my life to seeing their nation won to Christ. I was surprised, humbled, honored and overwhelmed with joy. Everything within me wanted to immediately shout a resounding 'YES' to their unexpected invitation. I wanted nothing more than to give the remainder of my life as a missionary in a foreign nation. This was the reason and motivation that brought me there in the first place. How could this not be God? After all, He is the One Who placed these desires in my heart. Although I did pray, I did so without any thought of hearing "NO" from the Holy Spirit. Then, I began designing a plan and strategy to embrace everything necessary to make this a reality. However, the more I planned, the more difficult things became until finally I knew God was saying "NO". Did the Korean leaders miss God in asking me to stay? Was I wrong in wanting to stay and be used by the Lord in their nation? Had I lost the ability to hear and discern the voice of my heavenly Father? Absolutely not! It just simply wasn't God's place or time for me or my family.

Just three years later (1978) we found ourselves packing everything we owned to move from Orlando, Florida to Bloomington, Indiana where I was being sent by the Lord to become part of the pastoral staff of a newly formed church in Bloomington, the home of Indiana University. Before leaving Orlando the chairman of the board of deacons in the church I had served in for the previous three years came to see me one last time. Instead of wishing me well, he began to boldly assure me that I had missed God and was supposed to stay on staff in that church. I sincerely loved this man who had been a godly influence in my life and a father in the faith to me. Nevertheless, even though in my flesh I didn't want to leave this man or his family, I knew without any doubt God had spoken and it was time to 'go'. What made the move even more difficult for us was where we were going. The church I was being led by the Holy Spirit to serve in didn't give any outward evidence of being a place where the Spirit of God could freely move and have His way among the people. Yet, the word of the Lord was unmistakably clear and I knew without any doubt I was to 'go'. Therefore, I obeyed His voice, said a final good bye to my friends at the church, and headed north. Within just a few days after arriving in Indiana I was blessed to lead two young men who were college roommates to Christ. Each of these young men were accomplished musicians and eventually became the first members of *Harvest* which went on to be used by the Lord to touch millions of lives throughout the world and leave a legacy of righteousness for others to follow. Praise the Lord!

Does any of this sound familiar to you? Have you ever argued with the Lord over things that you longed to do for Him and His glory? Have you ever been misunderstood and questioned because you made sincere attempts to do something that was directly in line with the Lord's gifts and anointing in your life, only to have God not release you to finish that which you had so passionately begun? If the answer is yes, then take comfort my friend in knowing that you are among the ranks of the millions of righteous men and women who have learned what it is to 'wrestle' with God.

The plans of the heart belong to man, but the answer of the tongue is from the Lord. Proverbs 16:1

When these instances occur in our lives all we can do is fall upon the grace and guidance of our faithful God. We can be confident knowing He will always be on the journey leading and guiding us, even though it may lead somewhere other than where we are presently looking. Be careful you don't become so preoccupied with the past and what *might have been* that you become sidelined and never finish the journey. *Draw near to God and He will draw near to you.* Trust in the promise that *the steps of the righteous are ordered of the Lord.* Continue to run the race with endurance and perseverance always allowing Him to be your Strength and your Encourager! *Faithful is He Who has called you, Who will also do it.* He is more than able to complete the work He has begun in you if you choose to continue in the journey. Don't quit now! The finish line is just ahead.

But we are not of those who shrink back to destruction, but of those who have faith to the preserving of the soul. Hebrews 10:39
For I did not shrink from declaring to you the whole purpose of God. Acts 20:27

Prayer

O my Father in heaven,

Help me to run the race without wavering You have chosen for my life and destiny. I long to be a vessel of noble use for Your bidding and pleasure. Too often I find that I have run ahead of You and Your plans. I pray those times will decrease and my times faithfully following in Your footsteps will increase. Please expunge from my heart and mind every distraction and disappointment that lingers from the past. In the days to come may every part of my character and conduct be given fully to finishing the race for Your glory and honor. Help me to run in such a way as to encourage others who have chosen to quit to once again trust You and re-enter the race with hope, confidence and assurance they will finish. Let no incident of life, pleasing or painful, ever have the opportunity to disqualify me from this race, this test in which You have placed me. You are the foundation of my hope, the refuge of my safety and the only means by which I can effectively run and win. Thank You for the marvelous things You have already done in my heart, my mind and my life. Once again I cry out, 'Not my will, but Yours be done'. I love and trust You with everything and everyone in my future. Thank You for Your promises that keep, guard, teach and lead me toward the goal of the prize of the upward call You have placed in my life through Your Son Jesus Christ. I am Yours and I run only for You. Amen.

The Story Behind the Song:

It was 1990 and the music of *Harvest* had been established for nearly ten years and by this time we had accumulated a large core of faithful followers. Now the Lord was challenging me to take the already established and well-accepted music of *Harvest* in a newer, more aggressive direction which would open the door for us to reach out to a lost generation of young people. As the Holy Spirit gave me the newer, more aggressive songs my excitement and expectation grew. However, the long standing support from the record company as well as several of our closest friends and supporters was not so encouraging. I was being challenged from every direction by several very influential people in the industry who were saying I had lost my mind and was about to destroy the ministry of *Harvest* by changing the music to a more aggressive format. To make matters even more difficult one of the longest standing members of *Harvest* was not onboard with the changes I knew God was commanding me to implement for the days ahead. Consequently, I began to second guess my decisions and falter in my confidence and faith. Then, one day the Holy Spirit came in like a North Texas tornado and gave me the song, *Run the Race*. In those next few moments as the song came to life I regained my confidence and an unwavering resolve to move forward in faith. It took several months and a several changes in our staff, but by the next year we were moving in a new direction musically. During the five years that followed we saw tens of thousands of young people commit their lives to Christ as their one and only Savior. Hallelujah! By the grace of God many of those young people have grown up to follow the Lord's leading into the ministry of the gospel of the Lord Jesus Christ.

Run the Race

(Song from Carry On project, music and lyrics by Jerry Williams)

Oh, I'm tired of fighting all these physical battles
For the spiritual control of my life
There's days that I win and days that it's so easy to lose
(I think) I'm losing my mind

I'm weary with the reasons that I'm constantly giving
To the people who keep seeing me fall
I've got to run to win to be free from the sin
That easily keeps dragging me down

Chorus:
I've got to run the race with the heart of the Lord
Got to run even when it gets hard

I've got to run the race with the heart of the Lord
Running in the race, I've got to run and never give up!

It's easy to believe in the things that you see
(Even) easier to live for yourself
But any fool knows you choose your own road
In the end it's either heaven or hell

Can't you see that choosing what you hope to be right
It'll never be enough in the end
The only way to make it to the end of this life
Is giving all your heart to Him!

Chorus

Bridge: (Spoken part)
Every one of us has been given a chance in the race of life
And as we each face the struggles and demands of running
We ultimately realize that the race set before us
Is far superior and too difficult
Our only hope of victory is to abandon our feeble attempts to continue and turn to the only One Who has ever (run and) won

Every runner in the race for his life
Has got to run with both the good and the bad
But you've got to keep on running if you're going to be one
Of the many who are there at the last

So, don't confuse your running with times to be turning
Your energy toward something else
You've got to keep it straight or you're gonna be too late
You'll never get another chance to run

Chorus

To run giving anything less than
your best is to forfeit the gift!

DAY 9 CAPTAIN OF THE DAY

In Him the whole body is united and held together by every ligament with which it is supplied. As each individual part does its job, the body's growth is promoted so that it builds itself up in love. Ephesians 4:16

Being born in 1950 obviously means that growing up for me was a far different experience than anything young adults I meet today can relate to personally. Most neighborhoods today are unexplored territories with precious few neighbors ever taking the time to even attempt to get to know each other. City parks have become specialized team event zones that are seldom ventured into by neighborhood children who are simply looking for a common place to spend the day playing. Instead, most kids today are overloaded with a plethora of gadgets and games all designed to keep them inside interacting with their video consoles turning their homes into virtual playgrounds with untouchable team members who live who knows where in the world. It all sounds and looks amazing, but some very important and essential qualities are being unmistakably lost through these modern parenting methods.

When I was a young boy the only reasons my neighborhood buddies and I would ever be caught staying inside would be if we were too sick to get up, the weather was really, really bad or we were grounded for some rebellious behavior (such as disrespectfully talking back to your parents). Otherwise, when we woke up each morning the first thing on our minds was getting outside as quickly as possible. Once out of the house we would quickly join up and start playing ball, riding bikes, exploring other neighborhoods or just hanging out in somebody's yard. It was always that way, and always understood whatever we did would be done all together. Therefore, our neighborhood was an open playground with almost every yard within several blocks being available for exploration and playing.

Another aspect of growing up in the 1950's & 1960's that is nothing like today was kids back then all understood and accepted they had responsibilities to help out around the house. Working was a normal part of our daily lives. When I say 'work' I don't just mean doing the dishes and carrying out the trash. I'm speaking of kids actually working to make some extra income which greatly helped their parents with such things as their clothes, shoes, school supplies, baseball gloves, bike tires, etc. When I was growing up I can't remember any kid not working at some job during the summer months. That was another reason the neighborhoods were so important. It was not unusual to see one or more of us pushing our lawn mowers through the neighborhoods looking for yards that needed mowing. In those days I would mow and edge your front and back yards for just $3.00. Because we worked for almost everything we owned, we were very careful how we treated our 'stuff'. Although we didn't have that much 'stuff', we still had a knack for making what little we did have somehow last for a long time. This paved the way for some incredibly creative adventures through the years. I remember many times when a simple plastic bat and whiffle ball would turn into an all-day marathon of home run derby.

During the hot west Texas summers a normal day would usually begin when all the guys showed up in my front yard early in the morning. As soon as everyone arrived the two guys who were the team captains for the day would toss a coin to see who picked first. Once the teams were picked by the two captains the games would began. Eddie and Jerry Moore lived next door, then just down the street were Tony and Danny Vail, Johnny Buchanan, Ronnie Holloman, Grady Boyd, Eddie Rackow, and finally the Shirley boys two blocks over. Oh yeah, my older brother Jimmy would sometimes hang out with us, too. There were a few more guys in the neighborhood, but this was most of the 'gang'. Some of the other guys who weren't able to make it as often included the Gatlin brothers who lived four blocks over, and little Timmy who lived four houses down from us.

For me those were the 'good ole days' when we learned the dynamics of how to be team members rather than loners. Every day the 'gang' had to deal with real life situations that taught us how to relate to each other on a personal as well as a corporate level. We quickly learned that whining just didn't work with the 'gang' and therefore, if we wanted to be picked early the next day we had better 'suck it up', quit the whining and get on with the game. That's a much needed lesson in this age of high-maintenance, whining immature believers who are consumed with their own personal problems and have no idea how to be a team member for the greater good.

I am truly grateful for having had the opportunity to grow up in the days when relationships were vital and friendships became bonds for life.

In John chapter 17 Jesus prays a specific prayer for each of us:

I ask not only on behalf of these, but also on behalf of those who will believe in me through their message, that they may all be one. Just as you, Father, are in me and I am in you, may they also be one in us, so that the world may believe that you sent me. I have given them the glory that you gave me, so that they may be one, just as we are one. I am in them, and you are in me. May they be completely one, so that the world may know that you sent me and that you have loved them as you loved me. John 17:20-23 (ISV)

I am fully aware that society is far different today and most neighborhoods and streets are no longer potential playgrounds. However, it's my prayer that we can soon find our way back to a time when visible relationships are more important than virtual connections and games. Unless we once again learn how to 'team up' (much like the old neighborhood days), then the possibility of ever becoming a unified force for the glory of God is dim and distant at best. The truth is we need each other! We need to learn how to love and trust each other to the extent no one is ever left out of the game. Even though we always had guys no 'captain of the day' wanted to pick to be on their team, in the end everyone was chosen and everyone participated in whatever game we decided to play. That's just the way it was.

I'll tell you what! Why don't you come over and hang out with us in the morning? The old gang is gone now, but there's a new 'gang' already forming and they're awesome. If you will give it a try, you can even be our new 'captain' of the day. What do you say? If you pick me, I'll show you how we used to play 'Home Run Derby'. Who knows, maybe you will hit the first home run. I hope to see you in the morning.

<u>Prayer</u>

Dear Father,

In this day and age where everything is fast paced and instantly accessible, help me to slow down and realize the incredible value and potential of every person I meet. You said in Your Word that I am to consider others as better than myself. I have been so influenced by everything in life to do just the opposite I am fearful of being more of a loner instead of a team member. I can see that You, Your Son and the blessed Holy Spirit are a perfect team. Place within my life those individuals who will diligently, but patiently help me to move out of my self-seeking lifestyle into one that supports and encourages others by every word and action I do or say. Remove from me the tendency to whine when things do not go the way I think they should. Help me to learn that in giving my life away for others I will be fulfilled in Your destiny for my life. In my competitiveness help me to spur others on to greater heights rather than steam roll them for my personal gain and goals. I still desire to be the one You choose to do mighty exploits as a member of Your team. However, I know that my desires can easily become self-centered and self-promoting. Therefore, set a guard over my heart to protect others from my selfish tendencies. I long to be all You desire me to be so others who come to know me will be blessed and increased in Your presence. As long as You are the Captain of the team, then it doesn't matter to me who else is playing next to me. It's good enough for me to just know You picked them the same way you picked me and we are all equal in Your sight. Amen.

The Story Behind the Song:

If We Don't Believe has proven to be one of the songs that has crossed generational lines and identified me with three generations of believers. I wrote this song while walking in the woods late one afternoon after seeing something that forever changed my life. I had been contacted by Melody Green who asked if I would take time and stop by Last Days Ministries to see something she felt the Lord had told her I needed to see. Melody had recently formed Americans Against Abortion (AAA) and I had been privileged to help her raise tens of thousands of signatures against abortion which we had recently laid on the steps of the Washington Monument in Washington, D.C. I ceased what I was doing and headed on over to see her. As soon as I arrived she motioned for me to follow her into a side entrance of the building where she then led me to a small private room. In the room were a few chairs and a single eight foot long table draped in a solid black table cloth. Lying motionless on the table were three beautiful, perfectly formed babies who had recently lost their lives through the ignorance and sin of legalized abortion. Melody had been legally granted custody of the babies for that day. I was instantly paralyzed by the shock of what I was seeing and stood in total silence gazing at the horror and travesty in front of me. The longer I silently gazed at the lifeless babies, the more my heart began to break. I'm not sure how long I stayed in that room, but eventually I left in the same silence I had stood for so long. As soon as I returned back home, I grabbed one of my guitars and headed out to the woods to cry out to the Lord. I was angry, but also deeply stirred in my spirit knowing God was trying to say something specific to me. As I cried out to my God I began spontaneously singing the lyrics that eventually became the chorus to *If We Don't Believe*. By the grace of God this song has continued to inspire and penetrate the hearts of those who love the Lord for more than thirty years. My hope and prayer continues to be that one day a God breathed Awakening will once again spread throughout our nation destroying the wicked schemes of the enemy who has come to steal, KILL and destroy every human being, not just helpless little babies.

If We Don't Believe
(Song from the Send Us to the World project, music and lyrics written by Jerry Williams)

People are crying, the children are dying who don't even know
We're killing by millions, brothers and sisters,
Our hearts are so cold
While Christians are sitting talking 'bout Heaven
And when they will go
The world and its people move faster and deeper
To a living death below

Chorus
If we don't believe how will they know,
How will they hear if we never go, O Lord, send us to the world
If we don't believe how will they see,

How will they know they can be free, O Lord, send us to the world

If we are light of the world then what right do we have to not go
He's given us power to conquer the hour so why don't we go
He's called us His soldiers given us orders to tear down the walls
We'll sing and we'll shout, we'll carry them out
And we'll offer them to the Lord

Chorus

Bridge:
You've gotta believe (3x)
Send us to the world
Believe! You've got to believe!
Believe! Send us to the world!

Chorus

A good name is to be chosen
rather than great riches,
Loving favor rather than silver and gold.
Proverbs 22:1

DAY 10 A LIFE WELL LIVED

The thief does not come except to steal, and to kill, and to destroy. I have come that they may have life, and that they may have it more abundantly. John 10:10

I was born February 20, 1950 to parents who came out of the Great Depression which started in October of 1929 and lasted until 1939. Even though my parents were only small children during the Depression, that brutally difficult time deeply implanted within them the erroneous idea that physical possessions are paramount to one's importance and influence in life. Consequently, through all the years I was blessed to have them in my life I learned very early that any 'gift' I bought, especially for my mother, had to be well thought out and never some cheap imitation of something better. In her mind the value of the physical 'gift' was a clear indication of how much I valued her in my life. It wasn't until she was radically born again in her early 60's that she began to understand physical possessions are rarely undeniable proof of one's importance or influence in life. Remarkably, I find today that the majority of those presently in their 60's (my generation) continue to measure and value the legacy of one's life almost exclusively through the abundance of 'things' they have amassed over their lifetime. These 'things' of which I speak are most commonly financial wealth, earthly honors (degrees or awards), land, collectable possessions, size and type of residence, etc. After all, isn't that what the American dream is all about?

I am confident in the above text (John 10:10) Jesus is not at all speaking about the American dream. On the contrary, living an ‘abundant life’ has little or nothing to do with one’s tangible possessions, wealth or accolades received among men. Those ‘things’ certainly have their place and purpose, and can be powerfully used by the Lord in establishing His kingdom through His people in the earth. However, God doesn’t need earthly resources to promote His abundance or establish His Kingdom through the lives of His people. What, then, is necessary to truly live an ‘abundant life’? The answer to that question isn’t difficult at all, but is rather quite simple with God:

But if God so clothes the grass of the field, which is alive today and tomorrow is thrown into the furnace, will He not much more clothe you? You of little faith! 31 "Do not worry then, saying, 'What will we eat?' or 'What will we drink?' or 'What will we wear for clothing?' 32 "For the Gentiles eagerly seek all these things; for your heavenly Father knows that you need all these things. 33 "But seek first His kingdom and His righteousness, and all these things will be added to you. Matthew 6:30-33

All that is required is a heart that sincerely desires Him more than it desires all the other ‘things’. God is searching for those who seek Him first each and every day, and are wholly submitted and committed to Him and His plan for their lives. It’s really amazingly simple: The degree one yields themselves to the Lord allowing Him to invest Himself *(His thoughts, His ways, His Word, His will, His heart, His character, His attributes, etc.)* in their lives will determine the degree of abundance they are able to achieve in their daily lives. The more someone commits themselves to Him and His ways will consistently be evidenced through a life that is lived lovingly, joyfully and selflessly.

Do nothing from selfishness or empty conceit, but with humility of mind let each of you regard one another as more important than himself; do not merely look out for your own personal interests, but also for the interests of others. Have this attitude in yourselves which was also in Christ Jesus. Philippians 2:3-5

Throughout my lifetime I have been honored to meet many precious souls who were (are) truly living an 'abundant' life. The presence of joy and heavenly strength that unmistakably flows from their lives is like an artesian spring that's not only visible, but highly contagious and inspiring. This 'abundance' that continuously exudes from their daily lives is something that can never be achieved through self-promotion, but is released and maintained through a life that passionately pursues God Himself. If this explanation doesn't currently describe your life, then all it takes to begin personally experiencing a life of 'abundance' is a willingness to change followed by a moment of sincere repentance. 'Self' is the real enemy of our souls and will always seek to dominate our time, thoughts and energy. In this moment make the decision to lay your 'self' on the altar where it must be unmercifully crucified. As you leave 'self' at the Cross of Christ, then Jesus Himself will joyfully place within your broken and contrite spirit His immeasurable abundance and dominate every chamber of your heart and mind. Oh, the joy and peace that will flood your heart and mind in Christ Jesus!

When delving further into the opening text (John 10:10) I discovered that the word 'abundantly' can also be translated *extraordinary, uncommon* or *over and above*. As I pondered this I immediately thought of a precious and unassuming man who significantly touched my life in a truly extraordinary way. God took this amazing man home in 2007, but to this day he continues to be one of the great treasures, influences and heroes of my life. It might surprise you to find out he never wrote any books, never recorded any songs and never had the opportunity to preach to the masses. I would imagine you could count on one hand how many souls he led to Christ in his lifetime, and to my knowledge he always declined when asked to be part of the leadership of any church or ministry. Even so, this otherwise unknown man was powerfully used by the Lord to impart the wisdom and love of God into a very limited number of souls during his lifetime, and by the grace of God I was one of those rare and privileged few. Oh, how I remember and miss the times we would sit for hours as he listened to the ramblings and cries of my heart. Without my even realizing, time after time he was used by the Holy Spirit to patiently guide me through some pivotal times with his practical and wise counsel. No matter how hard things got in my life, this extraordinary man continually encouraged me to believe our mighty God for the impossible. For more than two decades he steadfastly supported me in the purpose and destiny he knew God had placed on my life. The majority of those moments and seasons I experienced with this *uncommon* man took place long before God ever released His gifts and calling through me on a national and global scale. Who is this hero of the faith in my life? This *extraordinarily uncommon* man was Robert 'Bob' Galloway, my irreplaceable friend and father in the faith.

I first met Bob in January of 1977 when I moved my family from sunny Florida to Bloomington, Indiana. Bob had spent his entire life in and around Bloomington except for the time he served as a combat medic in the army. I had recently accepted an associate pastoral position in a newly formed independent church in which Bob and his wife Louise were founding members and from the moment we first met they basically adopted us into their family. What an amazing time and what an extraordinary couple.

Soon after our arrival in Indiana I found out Bob had a Texas sized reputation as a fisherman. He loved telling how he started fishing on his own when he was only six years old and would regularly get into trouble for going fishing instead of going to school. This really excited me because while living in Florida fishing had become one of the new passions of my life. Consequently, I made it a point to visit Bob as often as possible hoping to learn everything I could about fishing in Indiana from the widely acclaimed master. By the time spring mercifully arrived I was chomping at the bit to go fishing. Then the long awaited day finally arrived for our first fishing expedition, and what a sight it was as Bob pulled into my driveway early that morning. I came bouncing out the door proudly displaying all my Florida 'big bass' fishing gear which included several 7-8 foot ugly sticks, ambassador reels and 20 LB test line. Bob took one look at all that gear and instantaneously started laughing at the big, bad Florida fisherman who was going to show them a thing or two about how to catch 'BIG' fish. I guess I forgot to tell you how I had been talking some pretty heavy smack all winter about how big the fish were I always catch. When Bob finally stopped laughing he turned and asked, "What are you going fishing for...whales?" That drive to the lake took a lot longer than it should have as Bob continued to chuckle each time he glanced back at my fishing gear. Once we eventually arrived at the lake, Bob then pulled out his ultra-light fishing tackle which consisted of several small 5-7 foot rods and reels with 4 or 6 LB test line. Before launching the smallish flat bottom boat, he gave me one last jab about my gear and said, 'Let's see who catches the most and the biggest fish today.' By most standards I did really well catching eight or ten bass with the largest weighing up to four pounds. However, I sat and watched as Bob easily caught fifty or sixty fish of various kinds including the largest bass of the day weighing somewhere between six and seven pounds. You can just imagine what the ride home was like. The only other thing I will say is the next time we went fishing I showed up with brand new ultra-light rods and reels complete with 4 - 6 LB test line. After all these years I still prefer to use my ultra-light fishing gear. Thank you, Bob.

Over the next several years Bob and I went fishing more times than I can remember. While on those trips he taught me extraordinary things about being a better father and husband, loving God for Who He is, serving God out of devotion rather than duty, and of course fishing. To this day I can't recall a single time we were ever together when he would be negative about anything other than having to go to the doctor on rare occasions.

For reasons I never figured out he had a strong aversion concerning going to the doctor. Aside from that single area, his gentle, loving spirit was contagious to all who had the privilege of knowing him. He was always finding practical ways to serve those in need without their ever knowing what he was doing. What this remarkable man has invested in my life cannot be measured by numbers or scales, but undeniably carries great wealth in the Kingdom to come. Through his simplistic, yet profound life I learned in greater depth the true meaning of love, joy, peace, patience, kindness, gentleness, self-control and godliness. This precious man of God mentored me in areas I had somehow overlooked in my pursuit to leave a legacy for the glory of God through the ministry. I can honestly say I am far richer, wiser and stronger today because of the 'investments' and 'deposits' unselfishly made into the personal account of my life through this amazingly *uncommon and extraordinary* man who most of the world never had the privilege of knowing.

Bob was eighty-five years of age when he graduated to be united once for all with His loving Savior, Master, God and Friend. Before he left this world I made one last trip to visit him in his home in Bloomington. I was with him two days, and once again I was without question the one who 'received' far more than I was privileged to 'give'. As I was leaving him the first day of my visit he said something that took me totally by surprise, 'I thought we were going to go fishing?' I turned and looked at this man who was already in the care of Hospice and said in a somewhat startled voice, 'You really want to go fishing?' He then replied, 'I want to go one last time with you.' He then told me the real reason he wanted me to take him fishing: 'You may think this is silly, but I want you to baptize me.' I was overwhelmed by his request and told him I would be honored to take him fishing and baptize him the next day. (I am sitting here holding back the tears as I write this account of one of the greatest days of my life.) I picked him up around 9:00 the next morning and we drove to a small private lake about twenty minutes down the road. I won't give you all the details of how difficult it was to physically make this happen, but thankfully I was somehow able to get him in the boat and miraculously we started fishing. Then, of course, the master fisherman started catching fish. All I could do was laugh and say over and over, 'Thank You, Jesus!' I watched the 'master' as he instinctively did what had become an unconscious natural part of his life. The joy that filled his face and spirit was priceless. Finally, after two and a half hours I said, 'Bob, we have to think about quitting so we can get you something to eat.' He reluctantly agreed and within a few minutes we were heading back to the dock. I had purposefully brought some things for the baptism and on the way back (I was rowing the boat) I shared with him how earlier that morning the Lord had shown me some amazing things concerning baptism, things I had never considered before. As I passionately began sharing the Word of God with him he did what he had so often done before, he started chuckling at me. He did this because I was literally preaching to him while sitting in the small boat. We both had a good laugh, then I prayed over him as I prepared him to be baptized. Immediately after I had baptized my dear friend we remained there lovingly embracing each other as a father and son quietly weeping together before the presence of the Lord. We both knew this would be our last embrace, our last fishing trip, our last day together in this life. As I prayed over him one last time I quoted Acts 20:32 (the same verse I had spoken over my mother seconds before she went on to be with the Lord),

And now I commend you to God and to the word of His grace, which is able to build you up and to give you the inheritance among all those who are sanctified.

I don't remember much about the short drive back to his home. Once I had everything back in place I hugged him one last time. Bob's spirits were high and there seemed to be a relieved expectation in his voice as we said our final 'good bye' in this world. We both knew with certainty his remaining days were few and his future secure. There were no moments of fear, regret or concern in his voice, but only that amazing smile still on his face. As I pulled out of his driveway knowing I would never see him again in this world, I was overwhelmed with gratitude to the Lord for having had such an extraordinary man in my life. I paused and quietly looked at my old friend's home one last time before I slowly pulled away. My continual joy is I have no doubt I will soon see Bob again in the Kingdom to come and will joyfully have an eternity to prove to him I can catch bigger fish than he can.

However long or short our days may be, I pray we all learn to live them with the *uncommon, extraordinary* 'abundance' that was so prevalent in the life of Robert 'Bob' Galloway. If I have ever been confident of anything, I am certain of this one thing, that when Bob stepped through the veil of this momentary life into the presence of God he heard the Lord say to him with a smile on His face, "Well done, good and faithful servant! Do you want to go fishing with Me today?"

<u>Prayer</u>

Dear Father,

Help me to never again be common or ordinary, but to walk in that extraordinary 'abundant' LIFE that is found only in You. Oh, how I long to live each day of my life pleasing You in every way, and proving my love for You in everything I do and say. May others have no other recourse but to identify my life as one that is uncommonly committed to You. Sweet Holy Spirit, please grant that I might increase in my love for You and thereby manifest Your love to all those I encounter in my life. Order my steps and guard me from choosing the ordinary, common way which offers no challenge and demands no radical faith. Make me more and more like Jesus. May the countenance of my face reflect the Light of Your glory and my lips be as a resounding cymbal continuously giving You extraordinary praise. May all who see me see Your likeness, love, tenderness and benevolent character in me. I am ever aware of my propensity toward choosing that which would pamper and coddle my flesh. Consume my heart and mind with joy for Your commandments that even though I am weak, in You I will find supernatural strength. Amen.

Hear Ye the Master's call, 'Give Me thy best'.
For be it great or small, that is His test.
Do then the best you can, not for reward.
Not for the praise of man, but for the Lord.

Every work for Jesus will be blest,
But He asks from everyone his best.
Our talents may be few, these may be small,
But unto Him is due our best, our all!

The Story Behind the Song:

A true 'friend' is a gift from God that is not only rare, but irreplaceable. To have more than one such 'gift' of God in your lifetime is to be 'abundantly' blessed indeed. I am one who has been so honored and blessed. 2007 was the year I lost my dear friend, Bob Galloway. That was hard enough, but in that same year I also lost another 'true and dear' friend and brother in the Lord, Alan Smith. Alan and Cherryl had been part of our lives and ministry since 1982 and were literally 'family' to us. Alan had been battling cancer for seven years and would soon be going home to be with the Lord. Thankfully I had the privilege to spend several days with him before he graduated. During that time I had the amazing privilege to sing over my dear friend, and *Well Done* was one of the songs I sang in those precious few moments. As I sang this song over his life, he sat quietly crying tears of gratitude and joy as he knew the Lord was telling him 'well done, my son'. Men are created with an undying drive to leave a legacy, fulfill a purpose and live a life that 'matters' in the end. Through the lyrics and music of this song the Lord powerfully assured Alan he had fulfilled his purpose and it was now time to come home.

Since 2007 I have had the distinct privilege to sing this song over a few others who were about to cross through the veil and forever be with the Lord. With so many lives being squandered and wasted through selfish endeavors and ignorance, I have truly been honored and blessed to have known a few extraordinarily uncommon people who unselfishly left a legacy for the glory of God. *Well Done*, Bob. *Well Done*, Alan. See you both soon.

Well Done

(From the project Thank You written by Jerry Williams from Matthew 25:14-30)

I can see just up in front of me there stands an open door
I don't know what lies beyond it, but this I know for sure
If I stay right where I'm standing now or turn the other way
I will never know what might have been and never hear You say...

Well done good and faithful servant! Enter in My joy!
Well done you have shown you love Me far above all else.
Well done now a multitude of others know My name.
Well done My child. Well done.

So with a strong anticipation I'm taking that first step.
You can come along and follow me, but I'm not going to wait.
'Cause up ahead there lies the answers to the reason for my life...
So get up...it's time to go! I just can't sit here 'til we die!

Chorus

Bridge
The crown of joy You've placed upon my head I don't deserve.
'Cause anything I've ever done for good was by Your love.
Whatever praise that men might choose to place beside my name
I cast it down with any crowns just to hear You say...

Choru

His lord said to him, 'Well done, good and faithful servant. You have been faithful over a few things, I will make you ruler over many things. Enter into the joy of your lord.
Matthew 25:23

DAY 11 THE REASON FOR THE SEASON

For unto us a Child is born, Unto us a Son is given.. Isaiah 9:6

It's no secret to those who know us personally that the weeks between Thanksgiving to the end of December are always our favorite time of the year. To be honest, we just simply can't understand the 'Bah! Humbug!' attitudes of so many of our brothers and sisters in Christ who seem to never really get into the Spirit of Christmas. For us, we sincerely love having a specific time each year when we can go all out openly celebrating the birth of our Savior without anyone thinking we are fanatical, crazy or weird for doing so. Think about it! From Thanksgiving until December 26th the whole world without even realizing it sets its focus and attention on the birth of ONE little Child Who is Emmanuel, God with us! I am well aware of all the other marketing garbage that goes on during the holidays, but even so, that still doesn't change the fact that Jesus is the Main Reason for Christmas! Without Him there would be no celebrating, no lights, no jingle bells, no Rudolph the red nosed reindeer, no Christmas trees, no Salvation Army volunteers standing in front of every store in America ringing their bells, and no time when the majority of society becomes focused on giving special gifts to friends, family and loved ones. That's why each year during this wonderful season we purposefully intensify our resolve and commitment to unashamedly and joyfully celebrate Jesus!

For God so loved the world He gave His only Son, that whoever believes in Him should not perish, but have everlasting Life. John 3:16

Hallelujah! What a glorious truth that the Child came to become the Savior to any and all who receive Him into their hearts by faith (John 1:12). It's also true He came to rescue His Bride and one day present her to the Father *without spot or wrinkle or any such thing*. What a magnificent season for us, the Bride, to rejoice in Him Who is our glorious, magnificent and soon coming Bridegroom. He came as the infant Savior of the world, but also as the Bridegroom of heaven to save and rescue His Bride.

Knowing this TRUTH intensifies and solidifies my resolve to openly celebrate Jesus during this time each year. How can anyone who hears this GOOD NEWS not instantaneously be motivated to celebrate? He came to save, deliver and rescue us, and then did just that! Hallelujah! He came because He unconditionally loves us and delights in us more than we have ever imagined. Listen as the Bridegroom speaks from His heart to His beautiful Bride:

Thou art all fair, my love; there is no spot in thee. Song 4:7

Do you realize He is speaking to you and me? How can this be? The truth is, this Child came with a view of eternity already firmly fixed in His heart. That's why He endured everything with joy knowing that one day He would present His glorious spotless Bride to the Father in heaven. Oh, what a reason and what a season to celebrate! He has already seen the end from the beginning and already perfectly sees what we will be as though it is already done. Oh, if during this season that sparkles and glitters we could but for a moment see ourselves the way God has seen us from the beginning. Oh, if we could only truly understand He is not angry with us (who have repented and turned to Jesus as our Savior), even though He knows all our wanderings both past and yet to come. He came to save, sanctify and ultimately glorify His

Bride. Oh, what royal delicacies await us at the Wedding supper the Father will hold for the Bride and her matchless Bridegroom! Oh, what a reason to rejoice! This is the season to be joyful!

Maybe you are one of those who have simply never paid much attention to everything I'm talking about right now. Maybe your past experiences during the Christmas holidays are not those that conjure up happy, warm feelings. If so, then I am sorry and pray all your future Christmas's will be filled with joy and expectation for the day when the Bridegroom of heaven returns for His glorious Bride. As for me, my earliest memories of Christmas are very nearly movie theme material wherein all the dreams of a little boy miraculously came true at the same time every year. It would always start on Christmas Eve with us celebrating my older brother Jimmy's birthday (what a bummer being born on Christmas Eve). Then, long before our usual bedtime, our parents would send us all to bed convincing us Santa Claus wouldn't come until we had all gone fast asleep. That's the only night of every year I can actually remember trying to fall asleep early. Then, usually around 5:00 a.m. the next morning while it was still pitch dark outside, our parents would wake us up proclaiming Merry CHRISTMAS! I can still remember the feelings of exhilaration as we would all leap out of bed and race to the living room.

Amazingly in the middle of the night our little home had been mysteriously transformed into a winter wonderland that was now brilliantly glistening from the lights on the tree and dozens of little candles that had been lit throughout the entire house. I will never forget those sights, sounds and smells. To a little boy it was like entering into a magical world where everything was dancing and sparkling in wondrous, heavenly light. It wouldn't take long before my eyes would be drawn to what looked like a truck load of toys under the tree. I remember asking, 'Where did they come from? How did they get in the house and I didn't hear anything?' It was never very long before all the presents were opened and we were showing each other our amazing presents arguing as to who got the best gift. To be brutally honest there were a few times I remember wishing I had received one or more of the toys my brother received. Since he was older, sometimes his gifts were bigger and more advanced than mine which made me a little envious. It all worked out, though, since we shared a bedroom.

Of course, as a little kid I didn't really grasp the full meaning of what Christmas was all about. However, I never questioned that it was all about God sending His own Son as a little baby, and that Jesus was born in a manger and came to earth because He loves me. Consequently, since God gave the greatest of all Gifts at Christmas, we were also giving each other gifts in honor of the Baby Jesus. Thank You, God! It's unrealistic to expect any young child to fully grasp the true reason for the season, but I've certainly never seen any small child who wasn't thrilled and full of joy during the season. There's just something special that grips the world during this time of year, and it's all because of Jesus.

The Christmas holidays also ushered in some other challenges, many of which manifested in some really ugly behavior from those who were my extended family. I grew up in a broken family which made getting together for the holidays a massive challenge that far too often turned into volatile encounters between estranged family members. For some reason these ugly outbreaks would occur more frequently during the Christmas season. I still have vivid memories of being snatched from the table full of amazing delicacies as my parents would be forced to leave because of the ugly attitudes of others in the family. Even still, the memories that continue to dominate and fuel my love and excitement for Christmas are those of the toys, food, fun, music (there's no other music like Christmas music) and my all-time favorite, homemade pecan pie.

As I grew older the true meaning of Christmas began to have a greater and greater impact on my life. I can honestly say that Christmas had a great deal to do with my eventually giving my life to Christ. Had it not been for a time of the year when everything around me pointed toward heaven and the reality that 'unto us a Child is given', I may never have known the real reason for the season.

May we all be blessed with heavenly vision to fully realize that while we were yet sinners Jesus willingly came to us, died in our place, was raised and is coming back for us! Hallelujah! He will certainly finish the work He has begun in preparing His Bride (us) for the great wedding ceremony and feast. Turn your eyes away from gazing on your faults, flaws and failures of the past year and see yourself with His eyes. That is the reason for the season. That is why He came and that is why we celebrate. Joy to the world the Lord is come. Let earth receive her King and the Bride receive her Bridegroom!

Prayer

O my God and Father,

When I think of all You have made possible through the indescribable Gift of Your Son, I am filled with ten thousand inexpressible thoughts and joys. Thank You for loving me with an everlasting, unconditional perfect love. Your love freely given to me has no greater expression than a life willfully returned to You through loving submission, praise and service. With all my heart I love and praise You for this Life You have freely given me. I was hopelessly lost and eternally damned until Your love came forth into this world as a little Child and rescued me from total destruction and everlasting darkness. But for Your love I would have never known the sounds and joys of heaven that now resound in my heart. But for Your love and boundless mercy I would have remained a prisoner to my sin and iniquity. Because of Your love I am no longer a prisoner of hell, but am now a grateful bond servant of the One Who is LOVE, Jesus Christ. May the shallow sounds of exploitation and the pursuit of mammon never drown out the joyful sounds of praise that are everywhere at this time of year. May I never get my eyes on the momentary and become cynical, but rather keep my eyes on the eternal and be a continuously celebrating witness of Your love. You are my Light and my Salvation, my defender and strong tower. Therefore, whom shall I fear as long as You are with me. I love You above all my powers to express Who You are and what You have done through Jesus, my Lord and Savior. Amen.

The Story Behind the Song:

The only story behind the song *We Sing Glory* is my long standing love for Christmas. Being a musician, minister and psalmist, the purest form of expression I can give is writing an original song that captures the moment as well as the meaning of whatever I am presently experiencing in the presence of our mighty God. Because I have purposefully chosen to make Christmas a time of celebration each year, then it was only a matter of time before my experiences during this wonderful season would manifest through my God given gifts and talents. Through the years I have been blessed to write several songs expressing my love, joy and belief in *The Real Reason for the Season,* Jesus Christ! *We Sing Glory* is one of these 'experiential' songs which I wrote while in the midst of decorating our ministry campus one year. One day while I was fully absorbed in making decorations the joy of Christmas simply overwhelmed my heart. All I could do was shout GLORY! That led me into considering the magnificent scene that continually exists around the throne of God wherein myriads and myriads of the heavenly host are continually singing and shouting GLORY TO GOD IN THE HIGHEST! It didn't take long after that for me to find my guitar and begin writing music to express what I was experiencing in that moment with the Lord.

Oh how I long for the multitudes who live in danger and darkness in our cities and nation to find *The Real Reason for the Season* and come to know the JOY that fills my heart every Christmas. Oh how I long for the day I stand with my children and all together *We Sing Glory*!

<u>We Sing Glory</u>

(A song from the Warriors Arise project, music and lyrics written by Jerry Williams)

We sing glory, glory, Glory to God in the highest!
(We sing) Glory, glory, Glory to God on high!

We sing glory, glory, Glory to God in the highest!
(We sing) Glory, glory, Glory to God on high!

There will be peace on earth, among all the people of God
For a Child is born, Who will save us!
There will be peace on earth, among all the people of God
For a Child is born, A Son has been given to us, Oh praise the Lord!

Repeat entire song

For a child will be born to us, A Son will be given to us; And the government will rest on His shoulders; And His name will be called Wonderful Counselor, Mighty God, Eternal Father, Prince of Peace. There will be no end to the increase of His government or of peace, On the throne of David and over his kingdom, To establish it and to uphold it with justice and righteousness from then on and forevermore. The zeal of the Lord of hosts will accomplish this.
Isaiah 9:6,7

DAY 12 THE DOG DAYS OF SUMMER

But as for you, brethren, do not grow weary in doing good. 2 Thessalonians 3:13

I was just like every other kid growing up in the 1950's and 1960's who couldn't wait for the end of every school year to come and summer to mercifully finally arrive. Summers in those days were always a blissful respite from the nine long months of monotonous schoolwork. It didn't matter that the arrival of summertime brought with it the realization that we had to 'work' (it was common in those days for anyone old enough to go to school to be working at some kind of regular paying job during the summer). Even so, we still couldn't wait for those three glorious months of freedom to arrive. Needless to say, it was a radically different world back then from what is representative of a normal summer in the lives of today's young people. I, for one, actually looked forward to working every summer because it gave me a sense of responsibility, put a little money in my pocket, taught me how to value things and people, gave me a measure of honor in the family, and taught me how to respect and honor my elders (who were paying me). Plus, working kept me active during the summer months which in turn helped to keep me out of trouble, something I was good at finding whenever I was idle. Honestly, I can't remember a summer when I didn't work at doing some kind of paying job, but that never diminished in any way my excitement each year as summer finally arrived.

Amazingly there always seemed to be more than enough time to work, play summer baseball, help out around the house, go on a summer family vacation and still accomplish just about everything else I had been dreaming about doing over the twelve weeks of summer.

That's right, summers in the 'good ole days' (1950's & 60's) were always three full months and typically began around the end of May. For all the guys who made up the neighborhood 'gang' (all my buddies from the neighborhood I played sports with, went to school with, went to church with, worked with, etc.) every summer always started the same way. We (the 'gang') would first compile a common list of things we wanted to do that summer, which always included a few new and crazy ideas that seemed to get bigger and crazier every year. It never took very long, though, before we had thoroughly exhausted our new and grandiose ideas, which then caused us to reluctantly fall back into the same old tried and true activities we had done every other previous summer.

This reoccurring theme usually took about six weeks before the initial excitement wore off and the new ideas were fully dead and buried. That's when the inevitable monotony began to set in and the long, hot, dry days of summer took over. You need to understand this was long before refrigerated air conditioning was in every building or kids would spend the day hanging out at the mall. Malls hadn't even been built yet! Wow, am I old now! Consequently, what free time we did have was usually spent playing baseball or some other sport. Otherwise, we could usually be found roaming about the neighborhood like a herd of Hereford cattle looking for some shady spot to lay around. For some unknown reason the 'gang' would eventually end up in my front yard lounging under any shaded area they could find. What a sight we must have all been laying around sweating and talking about a bunch of nothing.

Invariably it was during those hot, lazy, humdrum days we would concoct some new and crazy idea that would generate a whole new energy and excitement that usually lasted until school started back up.

Travel back in time with me to the summer of 1963. Of all things kites (Yes, I said kites) had become the big craze that particular summer. I know that doesn't sound very exciting, but it's what we did with the kites that made that summer stand out from so many others. Being status quo and doing what everyone else did never really worked for the 'gang'. Therefore, there wasn't a chance in a thousand you were going to find the 'gang' spending our 'free' time simply holding onto a string and watching a kite lazily float in the sky. Can anyone say, BORING!?

From the moment we acquired our kites we instinctively began experimenting with them to see how we could make them go higher, dive more dramatically and respond to our control more effectively. That's when I concocted one of my many 'crazy' ideas (these ideas more often than not landed us in trouble with several parents around the neighborhood). So what was this ingenious idea that made that summer one of the most memorable? It was the creation and instituting of Kite Wars! What a brilliant idea! The single objective of the WAR was to seek and destroy the other guy's kite until only one kite remained victoriously airborne. I quickly figured out the quickest and most effective way to eliminate the competition was to break or sever the enemy's kite string.

It wasn't long before I had engineered a way to carefully secure razor blades in the wooden edges of my kite frame. Once this was successfully accomplished and became a working reality, I would simply maneuver my kite across anyone's unprotected kite string and the next second they were chasing down their vanquished vessel. I rarely lost the WAR, but victory didn't come without a price. Time after time as I would masterfully slice through the line of someone's kite, the vanquished kite would invariably land squarely on top of one of the neighbor's roofs. Oh well, victory always comes at a price. However, my biggest issues came from the parents of the younger boys who would run home crying to Mommy after I had vanquished their prized kite. I know that sounds mean, but it was WAR!

The very next summer began with the 1964 summer Olympics. Needless to say the whole 'gang' got really motivated to become the next great future Olympic stars. Not surprising, we came up with several more awesome and 'crazy' ideas. One of the first 'new' ideas (inspired by the Olympics) we incorporated into our summer activities included the use of an old stinky, worn out mattress I found lying in the alley. I figured out it could be the perfect landing area for a neighborhood pole vaulting pit (pole vaulting was one of our favorite sporting events in the summer games).

After some lengthy deliberations we decided to bury it just under the surface of the ground directly in the middle of the alley. We were able to do this in such a way that didn't interfere with the trash truck which came twice a week to pick up the trash. Once the mattress was ingeniously buried, we then took some 2 X 4's we had laying around and secured them vertically in the ground on each side of the alley. Then we took another long board and ripped it (cut it in half length wise) to create the all-important bar needed to jump over. The only thing left to complete the pit was to dig a hole in front of the pit to plant the pole in as we attempted our jumps. Now that the pit was completed, all that remained was finding a pole long and strong enough for us to make our vaults.

It wasn't long before I had commandeered a ten-foot aluminum pole that was perfect (I still can't remember where I got that pole). All throughout that summer you could find the 'gang' out in the alley jumping over and over trying to set new records. That summer we must have all jumped a thousand times and amazingly no one ever got seriously hurt, although there were a lot of scrapes and bruises.

There were dozens of other crazy ideas that bombed soon after they were attempted, such as the time the 'gang' dug an underground cave in a nearby empty lot. It was going to be our secret hang out and worked great until the first heavy rain came. The whole cave collapsed leaving a huge hole in the ground and getting the 'gang' in a lot of trouble from the owner of the lot. Thankfully no one was inside when it imploded. Then there was the summer we all decided to raise pigeons. One of our favorite things to do was spend the night in the different pigeon houses and raid any nearby peach trees or watermelon patches. There's no stomach ache quite like the one you get when eating green peaches all night long to get rid of the evidence.

Whatever each summer brought there was one thing we always had in common - whatever we did, we did it together. We were inseparable. It's amazing how I can still see the 'gang' in my mind's eye as though it were just last summer when we were having Kite Wars or pole vaulting in the alley or spending the night in the pigeon houses throughout the neighborhood. As I reflect on those days from so long ago it's easy to understand now how powerfully they influenced my character and helped mold me into who I am today. I learned so many vital life lessons growing up with those guys, lessons that continue to have an impact on who I am today as a man, and as a minister of the gospel of Jesus Christ. It was during those dog days of summer hanging out with the 'gang' I learned how to be a team player, a friend and a leader. (Read Captain of the Day!) It is highly uncommon today to find real 'teams' in place in any local neighborhood, church or ministry that are functioning out of relationship instead of responsibility or duty. I see well-meaning wonderful people every day serving their church or ministry trying to take care of the ever present needs, but that's not what I am talking about.

When you consider the 'team' Jesus formed, they were 'comrades and friends' as well as disciples and servants of the Lord. They ate, prayed, played, ministered, laughed, cried and argued together. What most 'teams' in most churches and ministries today consist of are groups of sincere people who only come together during their meetings. Outside of these meetings they have no meaningful relationships or friendships with each other, but they still work hard at keeping something pumped up so it won't deflate and die. I adopted a little motto I heard from a preacher in the early 70's which says, 'Anything you have to pump to keep alive needs to die!' If we are ever going to see the power of God manifested in the earth through a true wave of God-breathed revival we are going to have to learn how to be a God empowered, God breathed, God appointed, God anointed 'team'. This kind of 'team' is based on relationship first, not responsibility or results. It's only when each part of His body becomes jointly fit together and begins to properly function that this kind of outpouring is going to be manifested in the earth and in our lives.

I don't miss the heat, the boredom or the uncertainty of those summers from so long ago, but oh, how I long for the camaraderie of a close knit 'gang' of guys who choose to do everything together. That's when the dog days of summer turn into unforgettable days of glory. Oh Lord, let Your glory fall again!

Prayer

My great and Sovereign Father,

I know You are no respecter of persons and favor none of Your children over another. I fully acknowledge how, in Your infinite wisdom, You have created us with individually unique qualities, but still with the purpose of being joined together into one complete body, the body of Your Son Jesus Christ. Too often my attention and energy is given to pursuing only that which I am created and able to do. I beseech You, my Father, enlarge the capacity of my heart to openly embrace my brothers and sisters in Christ knowing they are vital to the fulfillment of Your destiny in my life. Keep me from ever pursuing them solely for the purpose of promoting what I am doing. I realize I am in need of a radical and immediate change in order to become a spontaneous and beneficial team member. Help me to willingly and readily embrace my brethren in Christ. Enrich my life through their instruction, discipline and godly example. May I in turn be to them a spring of fresh water from Your presence as well as an inspiration to their lives to continue the journey with hope and perseverance. May we become a united team moving forward as one man with one heart and one purpose for Your glory alone. Amen.

Blest be the tie that binds...Our hearts in Christian love
The fellowship of kindred minds...Is like to that above
Before our Father's throne...We pour our ardent prayers
Our tears, our hopes, our aims are one...Our comforts and our cares.

The Story Behind the Song:

Oftentimes when I was in my songwriting mode I would clear my head by opening to the Psalms and singing the words in a creative song to the Lord. *Creator's Song* was birthed in one of those spontaneous moments when a dozen other song ideas were rattling around in my head. I have always believed that my best songs were written in the midst of the 'dog days' of writing when the Lord would suddenly invade my heart and mind and give me a heavenly song. It may surprise you to hear me express that I experienced 'dog days' when writing. I have written over 2,000 songs and have hundreds (if not thousands) of other song ideas that were never completed. Trying to come up with ten or eleven new and fresh songs for a new recording project each year was really, really hard work and took hundreds of hours of my personal time. I have written hundreds of songs that are good, but not great. However, there have been those few times when the Lord simply 'gave' me a song, and those heavenly songs are always timeless.

Creator's Song
(A song from the Voices project, music and lyrics written by Jerry Williams)

Worthy art Thou, O Lord our God
To receive glory, honor and power
Worthy art Thou, O Lord our God
To receive glory, honor and power
You have created and by Your will
All people on earth have their being
You have created and by Your will
They exist to bring You the glory

Chorus

From every people and nation on earth
You've purchased men by Your blood
You've made them a kingdom and priests to our God
They will reign on earth forevermore

"but, speaking the truth in love, we are to all grow up in all things into Him Who is the head, Christ, from Whom the whole body, joined and knit together by what every joint supplies, according to the effective working by which every part does its share, causes growth of the body for the edifying of itself in love."
Ephesians 4:15-16

DAY 13 DANGER IN PARADISE

Be sober, be vigilant; because your adversary the devil walks about like a roaring lion, seeking whom he may devour. 1 Peter 5:8 NKJV

It was fall of 1956 and dove hunting season had just opened in West Texas. Papaw (my grandfather on my mother's side) had just invited me to go hunting with him, but also made it clear I was still too young to start shooting a shotgun. He still wanted me to tag along if I wanted to and watch him so I could start learning how to hunt. Papaw was a nationally renowned master marksman with dozens of awards in several categories for his marksmanship, so even at my young age I understood that to be invited to go and actually see him in action was a special and rare invitation.

This was my first time to go hunting, so I couldn't wait to load up and go. The first thing I learned was that one of the best places to hunt dove or quail in West Texas was in the vicinity of a livestock watering hole. Usually these areas would be large above ground tanks with a noisy windmill that continuously turned helping to keep the tank full of water. On the way Papaw made sure to carefully explain to me everything that would be taking place when we finally started hunting. One thing he repeated several times was, 'Son, if you'll keep an eye on everything I am doing and stay close to me, then I will let you retrieve some of the birds I shoot. But you will have to make sure you keep your eyes and attention on me, and only go when I say go.' Wow! That was like giving cotton candy to a toddler. All I could think about the remainder of the short drive (about thirty miles outside of town) was chasing down those birds for my 'bigger than life' Grandfather.

Within moments after arriving at the watering hole the first flight of birds began to come in for water. I didn't see them at first, but heard Papaw call out, 'Incoming!' Boom! I must have jumped three feet off the ground when he fired that first shot. At times the action got so frenzied there were three or four men shooting birds at the same time. I didn't have a clue what birds belonged to what man. All I could do most of the time was stand next to Papaw with my hands over my ears. Then the moment came when Papaw said, 'Son, I want you to get the next bird I shoot, but wait for me to tell you when to go!' Within only a few seconds another flight of birds came racing in, and the Master didn't miss a single shot. Everything within me wanted to immediately bolt from his side and retrieve the birds, but he firmly said, 'Not yet! Keep your eyes on where the birds fell and you can go get them in a few moments.' Boom! Boom! Two more birds fell. Then, just as quickly as it started it was over and the only sound I could hear was Papaw reloading his double barrel shotgun. At that moment he said, 'Alright son, go get those birds.' I had done exactly what the Master told me and kept my eyes on the areas where each of his vanquished birds had fallen. Instantly I was off and running snatching up all three birds before racing back to his side. As I handed him the birds and looked into his eyes I could feel through his gaze and the big smile on his face just how proud he was of his grandson in that moment. Then he simply said, 'Good job, son.' Before I had time to bask in that affirming moment, Boom! Boom! It was all happening again just as before. This time there were a lot more birds and Papaw masterfully shot a couple that were much farther out than the first three I had retrieved. Again, as things settled down, he told me to quickly retrieve the birds. It was exhilarating running after the birds thinking only of where I had seen them fall to the ground. Suddenly, I heard Papaw's powerful voice commanding me to immediately stop and stand perfectly still. I had never heard him speak with such force before, but even though I didn't understand why he was speaking so strongly to me, I immediately obeyed and did exactly as he said. Confused, but standing perfectly still, I then saw why he had yelled so dramatically for me to STOP. Unknowingly I had run directly into a den of active diamond back rattlesnakes. As my eyes adjusted to my immediate surroundings I then saw at least a dozen rattlesnakes all around me. I was instantly paralyzed with fear as the sound of their rapidly shaking rattles began filling the air. Boom! Boom! Boom! Boom! The ground suddenly began exploding all around me as the Master opened fire. Boom! Boom! Boom! His shotgun just kept blasting away. The first shots perfectly targeted the venomous foes closest to me, then one by one the remainder of the dangerous serpents were destroyed until I was completely out of harm's way. Papaw came running to my side (I had never seen him run before) making sure I had not been bitten and the imminent danger was gone. He then took me by the hand and slowly walked me back to a safer area before returning to investigate the snake den one last time. After a short discussion with the other hunters, a decision was made to abandon hunting dove and continue hunting for more snakes in that immediate area. Amazingly, by the time it became too dark to see clearly the band of hunters had killed and collected thirty-two of the deadly rattlesnakes, with the largest being just over six feet long. It truly was a miracle that I survived that day, and wouldn't have were it not for the Master being with me.

When I think back on that remarkable day in my young life I realize how God in His sovereignty chose for me to become the grandson of Miles Jones, a world renowned master marksman. The Lord knew my life would one day be physically surrounded and threatened by deadly serpents. In perfect Wisdom He provided the perfect person to keep me safe in that deadly moment. It is absolutely true to say that I would not have survived that day had I not been at the side of an expert Master marksman. It took precision and expert skill in the midst of a life and death situation to eliminate the dozen or more diamond back rattlesnakes surrounding me that day. By God's grace I suffered no harm, and it was all because God had already provided a mighty warrior to protect me against an unseen and deadly enemy.

Since those early days I have had several other instances wherein I faced deadly circumstances, but each and every time the Lord provided exactly the right person or people who unselfishly stood in the gap for me. By His grace I have also been able to stand in the gap for others who were in danger or whose lives were under vicious attack from an unseen enemy. That's why it's always amazing to me when I meet people who are primarily negative all the time. You know what I mean, 'the glass is half empty' kind of people. Long before I had ever made a commitment to the Lord He was intervening on my behalf and protecting my life. He has been with me all the time and has promised to never leave me or forsake me. There will always be dangerous and deadly intruders threatening our lives in this world, but as long as we keep our focus and our attention on the Master, no harm will befall us and we will remain safe and secure. As we all learn to hear and heed the Voice of our Heavenly Master we will not only survive, but walk away from the place of danger with an unexpected bountiful supply of meat.

Are you in trouble right now? Have you unknowingly run headlong into a deadly place? Be still! Listen to the Voice of your heavenly Father and do exactly what He says. If you will, then I can promise you He will take out the deadly enemy and rescue you from this momentary peril.

Anyone want to go hunting with the Master Marksman today? If you do exactly what He tells you, then when it's all over maybe you, too, will hear Him say, 'Good job, son!'

Prayer

O my Father, and the Master of my heart, I am so grateful that Your never-failing providence orders and protects every step I take and every event of my life. Set a guard over my heart this day that I might not ignorantly run headlong into the place of danger and unnecessary peril. Teach me to patiently wait listening intently for the sound of Your voice directing and assuring me the way is clear. Deliver me from thoughts that hasten and heighten my fears and hinder my faith. Should I find myself in the midst of a serpent's den, surround me with songs of deliverance. Instead of becoming easy prey for the venomous enemy, may the bounty of his camp become the spoils that encourage and enrich the remaining days of my life. Thank You for sovereignly placing skilled and mighty men of valor around the borders of my life and family. May I never cease to give them the honor they are due while ever giving You the glory and praise for the provision of their friendship and protection. I love You my Rock, my Fortress, my Shield and Protector! With You fighting for me every foe will tremble in fear and must flee. Anoint my lips with the songs of salvation that I might forever shout of Your victory and might. I love You, Lord! Amen.

Behold, I give you the authority to trample on serpents and scorpions, and over all the power of the enemy, and nothing shall by any means hurt you. Luke 10:19

The Story Behind the Song:

The first dozen or so years I was a father were for the most part a breeze and most of the time a blast. Then, when my oldest daughter turned fourteen, everything changed. For the next several years our home became more of a war zone than a sanctuary or oasis. The majority of those days I felt more like a soldier on guard in enemy territory than a father looking to hang out and enjoy life with his family. In many ways those few years were much like the time I unknowingly ran into that den of diamondback rattlesnakes the above story documented. If you have ever parented teenagers, then more than likely you can relate to what I'm about to say. On many days while just going about your normal activities you suddenly find yourself surrounded on every side by a multitude of deadly things, and they all are coming from the 'teen zone' in your home. Don't get me wrong, we had a lot of wonderful days and many great victories. However, as soon as we would vanquish one den of rattlesnakes, another one more deadly and fierce than the last would appear out of nowhere and invade our lives. I can't tell you how many times I felt helpless and clueless as to what to do next. It was during one of these helpless moments when the Lord spoke to my heart assuring me that He was my Keeper and all I needed to do was completely trust Him (again) with my children and ALL their circumstances. Hands down parenting is the hardest responsibility I have ever been given by the Lord because it requires continuous unconditional love and forgiveness, something I didn't know how to walk in for many years. Thankfully, God never calls us to do something He hasn't made every provision for, as well as made a way of escape if it gets too difficult. I am still that soldier on guard to this day, but now I am fully trusting God to be my Keeper as well as the Keeper of my children and grandchildren. The enemy has done great damage through the years, but God is still in control having lost NONE of His KEEPING POWER. Hallelujah! If you are struggling as a parent of a child who has turned your home, heart and life into a war zone, then I pray these lyrics will encourage your heart and lift your spirit assuring you that God is your Keeper through it all!

God is our refuge and strength, A very present help in trouble. Therefore we will not fear! Psalms 46:1-2

You Are My Keeper

(Song from Give Them Back project, music and lyrics written by Jerry Williams)

When I don't know which way to turn, I know You'll protect me
When I don't know which way is right, You lead me on!
In the heat of the day You're always there to cover me
You are my Keeper! You are my Lord!

Throughout the seasons of my heart, You're always near me
Through the times of bitter cold You keep me warm
When the eyes of my spirit can't seem to clearly see You
You are my Keeper! You are my Lord!

Chorus:
So my God unto You I will sing!
My God unto You I give the glory!
With my heart, with my mouth I will give You praise!
You are my Keeper! You are my Lord!

When I don't know the reasons why, I know You'll teach me
And when I question what You've done, You never leave
Through the times of despair, times I can't hear You calling
You are my Keeper! You are my Lord!

Chorus

DAY 14 UNEXPECTED HONOR

How beautiful upon the mountains are the feet of him who brings good news, who proclaims peace, who brings glad tidings of good things, who proclaims salvation, who says to Zion, Your God reigns! Isaiah 52:7

We were in the third and most grueling week of an east coast tour and had already witnessed the Lord doing phenomenal things in the previous two weeks. We had just arrived in the beautiful mountains of West Virginia where we were scheduled to do a region wide concert at the local high school auditorium. Our expectations of seeing any kind of a crowd show up, though, were extremely limited due to an intense spring storm that had firmly entrenched itself over the region and had been pouring down buckets of rain for hours. Furthermore, it was the last leg of a month long tour, so everyone was physically and emotionally exhausted. As time for the concert approached much to our surprise hundreds of people began flowing into the Martinsburg High School auditorium. Needless to say this unexpected occurrence quickly re-energized every member of our team and greatly increased our belief that the Holy Spirit was going to do something extraordinary that night. Well, that's exactly what happened as God powerfully showed up and manifested His presence to all who were in attendance. I don't remember how many gave their lives to the Lord that night, but it was approximately one hundred young people and adults. What I do remember was it was one of those rare nights wherein it was literally raining inside (the Holy Spirit being poured out) as well as outside. Hallelujah!

As soon as the concert had officially ended I headed directly to the bus instead of staying on stage and mingling with the people (which was my normal routine). I had hit the proverbial 'wall' and was vocally and physically exhausted. Consequently, I quietly slipped out to find a place to rest while the team spent the next few hours breaking down all the equipment. By now it was raining even harder outside, so I was confident everyone would be preoccupied with trying to get home as quickly as possible instead of hoping to spend a few moments speaking to me. As usual our tour bus was parked out of sight in the back of the building which made it even more difficult to find me, especially in the pouring rain. Astoundingly, I had only been in the bus for a few moments when to my amazement I noticed a young man standing outside in the pouring rain staring directly into the bus at me. I couldn't believe it. He was just standing there completely motionless staring at me all the while getting totally soaked. I was so exhausted my first reaction was to look away hoping he might decide to leave. After a few seconds I turned to look again and he was still standing there not having moved at all. At this point I turned the interior lights on in the bus and motioned for him to quickly come inside out of the pouring, cold rain. As he ran up to the door it was only then I realized he was just a teenager. Even though he was soaked through and through from the pouring rain, it was obvious he was also crying. He declined my invitation to come any further than the entrance into the bus as he could tell I was exhausted and needed to rest. Standing just inside the front door he then said, "Mr. Williams, I am so sorry to bother you, but I really needed to take a moment and tell you thank you." Puzzled, I asked him his name and what he could possibly need to say to me that would cause him to stand in such a downpour until I finally acknowledged him. He very respectfully told me his name was Rusty, and then as the tears began to flow again he shared why it was so important to tell me, 'Thank you.'

We had been in concert at this same high school a year earlier, and Rusty had come then along with his best friend. His best friend had never shown any interest in going to church or living for Jesus, which meant he had certainly never been to a live Christian concert. Rusty explained, 'He told me he wasn't going to come at first, but I kept telling him he needed to come. Finally, at the last moment he changed his mind and decided to come with me.' Rusty paused and wiped back the tears again before he continued with his amazing story. His countenance and voice changed as he shared how, at the end of the concert a year earlier, his best friend unashamedly made a radical decision to accept Jesus as his Lord and Savior. Rusty excitedly went on to share how everything suddenly and powerfully changed in his friend's life, which also dramatically changed the dynamic of their friendship. They started talking about the Lord and going to church together. Then Rusty stopped speaking for a moment while staring down at the steps to the entrance of the bus. Then he said, 'Mr. Williams, just two weeks after the concert last year my friend and I were working on my dad's farm plowing the fields on the sloping side of the mountain, something we've done a hundred times before. I'm not sure exactly what happened, but somehow my friend lost control of his tractor and it rolled over on the steep mountainside. I helplessly watched as he was thrown from the tractor just before the plow rolled over him. Instantly both of his legs were severed from his body, and he was lying there with only moments to live. I leaped from my tractor and ran as fast as I could to his side. As I picked him up in my arms and held him not knowing what else to do, he looked up and with his last breath said, 'Thank you for making me go to the concert. I'm going to go to my Savior now.' Then he was gone. So, Mr. Williams, I had to find you and tell you, 'Thank you' for coming last year to our town. Had you not come I know I would never have seen my best friend again. Now I know I will see him again in heaven.'

I was speechless as I looked into the face of this amazing young man who had come to honor me for faithfully proclaiming Jesus to his best friend a year earlier. Then I realized his tears were not tears of sorrow any longer, but rather tears of joy. He told me 'thank you' one more time, shook my hand, then slipped back out into the pouring rain and was gone. I've never been back to that part of West Virginia, but I'll never forget the look on Rusty's face as he told me, 'Thank you' that night. As he departed I was the one who then bowed down and gave honor and glory to the Lord for giving me such a holy and lofty calling. Thank You, Jesus, for calling and anointing me to preach the Good News of the Gospel to those who would otherwise be perishing. I can't wait to one day sit down at the feet of Jesus with Rusty and his best friend. That will truly be a glorious time as we rejoice in the goodness and greatness of our awesome Savior.

Let not your heart be troubled; you believe in God, believe also in Me. In My Father's house are many mansions; if it were not so, I would have told you. I go to prepare a place for you. And if I go and prepare a place for you, I will come again and receive you to Myself; that where I am, there you may be also. John 14:1-3

Prayer

Dear Lamb of God,

Thank You for making it possible for me to believe in You, receive You, follow You and live for You in the hope of everlasting Life. Without Your sacrifice that opened heaven's door and made the Way straight for my entrance, there would be no foundation or possibility of Hope, but only a dark, hopeless expectation and end. Give me the strength and courage to live my life only for You that others who are without Hope may through all they witness in me find Life and Victory in You as their Lord and Savior. By Your mercy and grace You are now my Savior, Master and King. This abundant Life that I now live in You has brought more to my soul and spirit than I could ever have imagined or describe in written or spoken words. I am deeply burdened by the darkness I see in others who have not acknowledged their need of a Savior and called you're your name, especially those of my own household. Anoint me afresh with the aroma of heaven that would draw their hearts into the place where they begin to hunger and thirst for You to be their Savior, Master and King. Amen.

The Story Behind the Song:

I have been honored to be a minister of the gospel of Jesus Christ as a pastor, psalmist, musician and teacher. One of the underlying benefits of being 'sent out' in ministry is the constant confrontation with the multitudes who are bound in sin. As a pastor I am well aware how easily those in local ministry can become isolated from the darkness and depravity that has gripped our nation. Without realizing it local pastors can be lured into spending the bulk of their lives ministering to the needs of just a few saints ultimately neglecting their heavenly mandate to 'go into all the world and preach the gospel'. As I've traveled throughout the world the ever-intensifying reality of multitudes dying and going to a God-less eternity continues to fuel my passion and heart to 'stand on a mountain, wave my hands, tell all the people, tell every man'. *Decision Time* didn't come from one particular experience on tour, but is the culmination of years of ministering to thousands of individuals who came face to face with Jesus and either chose to follow Him or ignorantly turned Him away.

Although my days of concert touring have long since passed, I still war in prayer for the salvation of the lost in our world. There is coming a day when the Babe lying in the manger will return as our conquering King. On that terrible day His Sword will drip with the blood of wicked nations and all those who have rejected His unconditional love and mercy will be cast forever into the lake that burns with the everlasting fire of His judgment. This TRUTH is what motivated the words and music to this song. I am so grateful for stories like the one just mentioned in this devotion. Thank You, Jesus for allowing me to be part of Your Great

Commission to 'go' and 'tell' everyone the Truth that alone sets men free! To God be all the glory and praise!

Decision Time
(Song from the Let's Fight project)

I'm going to stand on a mountain, going to wave my hands
(I'm going to) Tell all the people, going to tell every man
God is gathering His warriors
To execute His anger and to do His word

Listen everyone to the sound of my voice
You better get ready, better make a right choice
Sinner wake up for the day of the Lord
Will send you to die for the deeds you have done

Chorus
Oh-h, it's time, time for a decision! Oh-h, it's time, time for a decision!

He will come in fire on a cold, dark day
To punish the world for its iniquity
The land will burn and the trees will die
Every man's heart will be terrified

The sun and the moon no longer will shine
Stars will fall, it'll be a sign
The heavens above, they will rattle and shake
And every man's heart will hide in the caves
Chorus

Bridge: (Recitation) Matthew 24:29-31

In those days the sun will be darkened and the moon will not give its light, and the stars will fall from the skies and the powers of the heavens will be shaken. And then the sign of the Son of man will appear in the sky, and then all the tribes of the earth will mourn. And they will see the Son of man coming on the clouds of the sky with power and great glory.

Chorus

Two will be working on the job that day
One will be left, one taken away
The trumpet will sound and the winds will blow
The day and the hour no single man knows

Listen everyone to the sound of my voice
You better get ready, better make a right choice
Sinner wake up for the day of the Lord
Will send you to die for the deeds you have done

Chorus

DAY 15 LOOKS CAN BE DECEIVING

Behold, I give you the authority to trample on serpents and scorpions, and over all the power of the enemy, and nothing shall by any means hurt you. Luke 10:19 NKJV

It was a beautiful summer day in Flint, Michigan, and in less than two hours we would be taking the stage for a concert in the largest church facility in the city at that time. The auditorium held 8,000 people and by the looks of things we were going to be ministering to a near capacity crowd. Everything was going smoothly, expectations were high and everyone on the team was excited to see what the Lord was about to do. Approximately twenty minutes before the concert we all gathered backstage to pray. Suddenly one of the sponsor's volunteer staff members bolted into the backstage area where we were praying and with an urgency in his voice he said, 'We have a serious problem in the foyer and need you to come right now'. We were all puzzled by his request because as the guest ministers we represented or held absolutely no authority to oversee any issues that might develop concerning the facility. Having no idea what was happening I went with the young man who quickly led me around the immense circular foyer that ran the entire circumference of the building. As we drew closer to the main entrance I could see from a distance something very strange. At first glance it looked as if someone had placed a very large black cone-shaped object directly in front of the doors leading into the main auditorium. This odd looking object was impeding the path of hundreds of people who were attempting to enter the auditorium before the concert was scheduled to start.

Needless to say, the whole scene was creating a state of confusion for the concert staff who had no idea how to handle the situation. Maneuvering my way through the crowd I positioned myself directly in front of the large black cone-shaped object. I quickly recognized it wasn't an inanimate object as I first thought, but was shockingly a person. However, this was not just any ordinary person, but was instead a seasoned witch from one of the many covens existing in that region at that time. For a brief moment all I could do was stare at what looked like a scene right out of a Disney movie. She was fully adorned in her coal black witch dress with at least a dozen dragon chains dangling from several places on her body. The strangest thing was how she had carefully positioned herself on the floor making it literally impossible to see any portion of her skin. Her long, jet black hair draped forward completely covering her face while streaming completely motionless down toward her lap. Her hands were carefully tucked into the long black lace covered sleeves leaving only the multiple dragon bracelets and chains visible. What a sight she was! No wonder there was so much confusion.

Following the leading of the Holy Spirit I immediately knelt down as close as possible to her left ear and began speaking directly to her. There was no response whatsoever, just deadly silence. In that awkward moment of silence, the people finally realized who I was and began to get even more excited wondering what was about to happen. Without hesitation I immediately acted on what I was confident the Holy Spirit was directing me to do. I laid down on the floor directly in front of the unsuspecting witch with my back flat against the carpet. Then, using my shoulders to crawl, I carefully maneuvered my head and shoulders into the middle of the witch's lap. With a boldness that only God can give I extended my head under the opening at the bottom of her hairline allowing me to come face to face with the witch. As I gazed up through the dark opening between her long coal black hair and her lap I then said, 'Hello, my name is Jerry and I'm the artist who is performing the concert tonight.' Suddenly two huge black eyes opened wider than the floodgates of Hoover Dam as the witch was completely overtaken by surprise and fear. In that instant heaven and hell collided as she realized a warrior of God was in her lap. I have to take a moment and be completely honest. I'm sure many of you are thinking at this moment, 'I would never do anything that crazy or ridiculous!' Well, I've always been what many might call a little crazy, but even this was beyond the boundaries of anything I had ever considered doing before in the ministry. Even now as I recall this amazing story I have to smile in amazement at how the Holy Spirit sometimes unexpectedly leads and directs our lives in paths we would never otherwise choose.

Now for the rest of the story. Within seconds the previously motionless witch was startled out of her trance-like state and on her feet offering no resistance whatsoever. Instead, she just stood there staring in disbelief directly at me. I knew by the Spirit she didn't represent any threat to any of us standing there, so I once again introduced myself and then invited her to be my personal guest at the concert. Surprisingly, she cautiously accepted my invitation and I triumphantly led her and the rest of the throng into the auditorium. I then purposefully sat her on the front row directly in front of where I would be ministering. As the Word of God went forth the seed of faith lying dormant within her spirit was activated by the Holy Spirit. By the end of the evening the strongholds of hell were broken off her life and she was powerfully set free and gloriously saved. Afterwards as the team was breaking down all the equipment I sat for more than two hours with this former servant of Satan. It was at that time I learned the details behind what caused her to end up sitting in the foyer earlier that evening. She had actually come hoping to find deliverance from the deadly covenant she had made with the devil so many years earlier. She had made the mistake of expressing to some other witches her desire to quit functioning as a witch and leave the coven. In retaliation the witches of her coven placed a curse on two of her family members who then mysteriously became sick and died. Reeling from the loss of her loved ones as well as her desire to be free from that kind of oppression, she made a frantic last minute decision to seek deliverance and freedom at a Christian concert. Just finding the courage to actually drive herself to the concert was hard enough, but once she physically entered the foyer she became paralyzed with holy fear and fell down in the exact place we first found her. Not knowing what else to do she assumed the cone-like position and went into a learned demonically influenced trance for safety. Praise the Lord she was set free and SAVED that night! The amazing rest of this story is how this precious sister (Kathy) went all throughout that region for the next several years proclaiming Jesus to those who were bound in witchcraft and Satan worship of any kind. Hallelujah! What a mighty God we serve!

Reflecting back on that amazing night I remember how quickly everyone assumed she was there as an ambassador of Satan to attack the concert. There was no way any of us could have known her actions were a desperate plea for deliverance. I am convinced had I not been in prayer before this situation took place I might have completely missed being used as God's vessel of deliverance to this servant of Satan on that fateful evening. In this day and age when so many are in need of deliverance and the freedom that comes only through Christ, may God help us to see beyond the obvious problems and become available conduits of His promises to all those who are desperately in need of Him. May we be 'treasure hunters' rather than 'trash collectors' to all those we meet and know. The magnificent and glorious truth is God looks on the heart and extends His hands of mercy and hope to anyone who calls on Him for help. Thank You, Jesus for Your indescribable gift of Life!

Prayer

Heavenly Father,

You Who ride upon the clouds far above even the approach of foe or failure, let me always remember when in the midst of momentary struggles that You are ever with me and for me. Thank You for disarming every power and authority that would usurp control of my mind and soul. You are my Deliverer, my Captain and Commander, my God, my Master and the Warrior King of my heart and soul. Any foe who chooses to advance against me must face You first. Hallelujah! Because You are ever for me, then it doesn't matter who may line up against me. I am destined to win because 'greater is He Who is in me than he who is in the world'. I fully accept and rejoice in the fact that Your protection and presence come with only one requirement, that I give You ownership and control of the rest of my life. I gladly do this acknowledging that one day with You is better than thousands elsewhere. I am ready to do Your bidding. I am ready to be Your messenger of hope to those in darkness. I am ready to continually testify of Your love, mercy, forgiveness, greatness and power that have gloriously set me free. When fear tries to paralyze me and keep me from going forward, I need only to set my thoughts on You and run to the safe and secure haven of Your love. There every fear is banished and every foe vanquished. Here am I, Lord! Send me! Amen.

The Story Behind the Song:

It was the late 1980's and our oldest daughter had just become a teenager. With that came all the challenges of parenting a beautiful young girl who was being bombarded within and without. As we looked for help and encouragement from our family in Christ we found an abundance of counselors, but little practical help as we faced real life issues with a strong willed child. Then I began to notice this scenario existed far beyond our personal experience and was rampant in the Church at large. In my desperate search for practical godly help I discovered a glaring problem in the Body of Christ in the West. We used to say it this way (although it's not politically correct to do so today), 'There are too many chiefs and not enough Indians'. It didn't take long before a righteous anger rose up in my spirit as I realized the great deceiver of the brethren had masterfully manipulated multitudes of believers into thinking that possessing a weapon (The Sword of the Spirit) would automatically make them a warrior of God. NOT SO! A THOUSAND TIMES NOT SO! Consequently, I began to cry out to the Lord to anoint me with songs that would WAKE UP THE SLEEPING CHURCH, and become a 'CALL TO ACTION' for the Church. *We're Gonna Take Hell* is one of the first songs the Lord gave me for this specific purpose. I wish I could tell you that each time we sang this song AWOL soldiers of Christ rallied and took up their armor once again brandishing their unconquerable weapons while storming the gates of hell. On the contrary, on several occasions performing this song almost incited riots among the otherwise nominal believers attending the concerts. Amazingly, that was actually an answer to my constant prayer that wherever we ministered there would either be riots or revival. I am still filled with a Holy Ghost passion to CALL TO ACTION soldiers of Christ and storm the gates of hell. There is an ARMY God is preparing that will one day RISE UP and TAKE BACK TERRITORY in the name of Jesus through the power of the Holy Spirit. Those who profess to be soldiers, but have no idea how to effectively use their weapon (the Word of God) will not be included in the ranks of this mighty, end time ARMY.

<u>We're Gonna Take Hell</u>
(Song from the Carry On project, music and lyrics written by Jerry Williams)

Down deep in the heart of the city at night
The devil is on the loose
So many people are caught in the web of his lies
They can't even see the truth

Tell me where are the soldiers of Light
Who will conquer the night and go set them free?
Where are the people of God
Who will stand and really believe?

Now it's the father of lies, all the armies of hell
They're trying to take control
And they're after the lives of every boy and girl
To deceive and then destroy

Tell me are you the soldiers of Light?
Are you ready tonight to go set them free?
Are you the people of God?
In your heart do you really believe?

Chorus:
We're gonna take hell by the blood of the Lamb!
Conquer every demon with a mighty command!
Lift our voice like the thunder and yell!
People of God, come on, we're gonna take hell!

Get ready to fight for the right to their lives
Get ready to take control
'Cause it's a matter of time before they run out of Light
When the devil has got their soul

Tell me are we the soldiers of Light?
Are we ready tonight to go set them free?
Are we the people of God?
Will we stand, will we believe?

We're gonna take hell by the blood of the Lamb!
Conquer every demon with a mighty command!
Lift our voice like the thunder and yell!
People of God, come on, we're gonna take hell!

Do not rejoice over me, my enemy! When I fall, I will arise! When I sit in darkness, The LORD Will be a light to me. Micah 7:8

DAY 16 A HERO'S TRIBUTE

HONOR YOUR FATHER AND MOTHER (which is the first commandment with a promise), THAT IT MAY BE WELL WITH YOU, AND THAT YOU MAY LIVE LONG ON THE EARTH. Ephesians 6:2-3

Early one morning long before any daylight had begun to appear, I was quietly reflecting on many of the wonderful things the Lord has done in my life. Suddenly the presence of God flooded my heart, mind and soul overwhelming every part of my being in a conscious and inexpressible joy. By the grace of God, I have experienced these heavenly visitations many times throughout my life in Christ. Each and every time these conscious heavenly visitations occur I am immediately and significantly strengthened in the inner man and always experience a resurgence of faith, hope and love. Without fail these visitations are followed by a period of time wherein I walk in a renewed strength that overwhelms every lingering weakness as my thoughts are infused with His infinite and eternal thoughts, and I am refreshed and renewed in His purpose, plan and mission for my life. I truly believe these visitations are momentary glimpses into what our life will be like with the Lord in the New Jerusalem.

On this particular morning as I sat basking in the glory of His presence, unexpectedly the Holy Spirit flooded my thoughts with long forgotten memories of an individual who impacted my life more than any other human being. I sat in amazement as decades of archived memories were resurrected and brought to the forefront of my mind. It was almost as though I was the only guest at a private viewing of an upcoming blockbuster movie depicting events both great and small from the life of an unknown, but none the less modern hero who tirelessly fought overwhelming odds to emerge victorious in life, love and faith. The epic saga running through my mind recounted seasons where this unknown hero suffered heartbreaking betrayal, devastating setbacks and personal loss. Yet, through all the pain, suffering and sacrifice there was never any thought of quitting or surrendering. On the contrary, this amazing individual lived with an unwavering determination to press on until the victory was certain. What a life! What a role model! What an honor to have this person's life intertwined and connected to mine!

Then I became deeply saddened as memories of a time when I, as a brand new Christian, ignorantly displayed a judgmental attitude toward the life of this amazing individual. In my blatant immaturity I unmercifully pointed the finger at the obvious areas of weakness still lingering in the life of this individual. All of my judgmental and condemning words were birthed from ignorance and a self-centered childish view of what I thought was real holiness. I was so self-righteous toward this person I completely overlooked the chapters that had already been written in the permanent ink of sacrifice and suffering. Thankfully and mercifully my season of disrespect and dishonor toward this heroic individual was short-lived as the Holy Spirit thrust me into the furnace of affliction quickly burning away the dross of self-righteousness and pride. It's amazing how one's view of someone else's life will radically change when you are required to walk in their shoes.

What a day that was in the presence of the Lord looking back into the extraordinary life of this modern heroine. It's a story of a young teenage girl who in the mid 1940's unwisely chose to run away and get married in an attempt to escape a bad environment in her childhood home. Before long there were three young children, an abusive alcoholic husband and no one else to help carry the burden of the life she had impulsively chosen. Although still very young, this young heroine made a courageous decision that few in her day would dare to even consider. She decided to dedicate the remainder of her life to improving and celebrating the lives of her three children rather than placing herself, her career or her life's agenda first. Therefore, to protect and promote the lives of her young children, she divorced her abusive, alcoholic and addictive husband, then set her face like a flint to see them have the opportunities in life she unwisely forfeited through her own wrong choices. Nowhere in history will you find a story of greater courage, sacrifice and love that exceeds this young woman's life.

My thoughts continued to race back in time as I vividly remembered one particular year I wanted to play little league baseball. I had shown signs at school of potentially being a really good baseball player, but I needed my own baseball glove to be on the team. The only glove I possessed was from my toddler years and was a hand me down then. It was not only too small, but also torn and weathered from years of childhood abuse. A new baseball glove cost around $30.00 back then, and my mother was already working nonstop to keep a roof over our heads and food on the table. Therefore, spending $30.00 on a baseball glove was an expense the family simply couldn't afford. Even as young as I was, I understood how spending that kind of money could wreck the whole monthly budget. Consequently, I put the thought out of my mind and was happy to continue borrowing other kid's gloves when we played ball. Without my knowing it, this selfless young heroine made the choice to begin studying at night to elevate her learning skills in order to advance on the job so she could make enough money to buy me a baseball glove. Within only a few months she was honored on the job and received a much deserved pay increase. This was just before baseball season started again, and wouldn't you know it, I got the new glove and joined the team. That season I led the team in hitting and home runs, neither of which would have happened had it not been for the sacrifices of this amazing young heroine.

It wasn't until I was an adult and a father that I began to learn of the brutal and seemingly insurmountable circumstances this modern day heroine faced throughout many of the years of her life. You've already heard that as a young teenager she dropped out of school, ran away from home, impulsively got married and began having children while working as an entry level nurse. Without a high school diploma there were no visible possibilities for any significant advancement on the job. Instead of just giving in to her circumstances, many of which existed because of her own unwise decisions, she dedicated herself to beating the odds no matter what the cost. Day after day she would spend hours at a time reading out loud the pages of medical manuals onto a small tape recorder. She would then play those recordings back time after time until the information became part of her thought process. After many months of this intense study routine she was given the opportunity to be tested on what usually takes years of education to learn. She astounded everyone and passed every test with honors. Over the next few years further advancement and honors would be awarded to this unschooled heroine until she was offered one of the highest honors in that particular field.

As my thoughts began to re-focus on the present all I could do was give thanks to the Lord for having had this amazing person in my life for so long. Yes, I got the baseball glove and excelled in the sport, but only because someone I had selfishly overlooked sacrificed their life to celebrate mine. So who was this modern day heroine? The bravest, most sacrificial, unselfish and hardest working person I have ever known, my amazing mother, Betty Jones Williams.

The last few years with my mother were nothing less than a glorious gift of heaven on earth. She was able to work with me in the ministry and became known to people all over the world simply as 'Granny'. She often spoke to me of the 'spirit' God had placed in me, and that it was the same 'spirit' He had given her through the lean and difficult early years of her life. She said, 'Son, God has given each of us the heart of an overcomer. So don't you ever think about quitting because it's not an option!'

'Granny' often marveled at the lack of courage and commitment in the lives of so many in leadership in today's church. It always bothered her that so many of the messages, songs, conversations and books today deal with people who are being overcome, rather than being overcomers. She never understood why we (the Church in the West) so readily celebrate failure by giving it so much attention. She was a no nonsense girl who on thousands of occasions stared failure in the face and each time declared, 'Not today! Not ever! In Jesus' name, mountain be gone!'

As I look around today it's easy to see how desperately we need some new heroes to rise up in this modern day of impotency in the Church. The Church in the West is overrun with a 'spirit of fainting' when we should be advancing and proclaiming the Lord Jesus through a 'spirit of overcoming and freedom'. Pastors and leaders spend little time 'working' the ministry and have settled into a lifestyle of maintenancing the ministry. God didn't anoint us to be 'maintenance men', but He called, appointed and anointed us to be His 'mighty' men in the earth. He said, 'You are the Light of the World!' Isn't it time for some new heroes to get together and through the power of the Holy Spirit invade the darkness that has blinded the minds of those in the world? If Granny were still here she would be the first one in line.

So let me ask you this question: What does God see in you that you have yet to see in yourself? He chose you when no one else thought of you. That makes you a prime candidate to be the next hero of heaven on the earth!

For you see your calling, brethren, that not many wise according to the flesh, not many mighty, not many noble, are called. But God has chosen the foolish things of the world to put to shame the wise, and God has chosen the weak things of the world to put to shame the things which are mighty; and the base things of the world and the things which are despised God has chosen, and the things which are not, to bring to nothing the things that are, that no flesh should glory in His presence. 1 Corinthians 1:26-29

Prayer

Dear Father,

You are the only great and true Hero of all creation, yet You have created US to be imitators of Your Life, Your love, Your character and Your heart. This is a high and holy calling and a life we cannot live apart from Your anointing and presence. I do not feel worthy of such a calling, much less capable of accomplishing all You have designed, destined and desire that I should be. You have sent me forth empowered by the Blessed Holy Spirit to be the extension of Jesus in the earth, the Light of the world. I must confess that too often the light coming forth from my life is dim and flickering rather than a blazing fire. I could easily be discouraged and disillusioned when considering my accomplishments and abilities. But, praise be to Your Name, You have opened the eyes of my heart to clearly see and understand a GOOD work is ongoing in me and You alone are the Author Who will bring what You have begun to completion! Thank You for starting a GOD work in me! Thank You for choosing me to be Your son, and allowing me to be involved in Your work in the earth. Thank You for showing me that in You I am strong. Thank You for filling me with Hope that continually assures me though I fall, in You I will rise again! Thank You for Your promise to never leave or forsake me, a promise which gives me confidence in those times I unwisely and foolishly wander into darkness and willful rebellion to Your Word. I once again lay my life upon the altar of Your mercy calling upon You to be the Great Enabler of my life. Holy Father, do the impossible and the unexpected through my life today. Teach, lead and empower me to do mighty exploits for Your glory in the earth. Give me the wisdom to never commit myself to those things I can accomplish, but rather be wholly committed to those things that find their origin in Your presence and power. May whatever I put my hands and heart to do utterly fail unless You intervene. By Your mercy, love and grace I am a prince of heaven, a son of God, an ambassador of righteousness, a royal priesthood, a chosen vessel and more than a conqueror through Jesus Christ my Lord! Amen.

The Story Behind the Song:

The Name of Jesus is a song I wrote to give honor and glory to the Lord, Master, Creator and Redeemer of my soul, Jesus Christ. In a similar manner, I am offering the lyrics of this song in honor of the amazing life of my mother through whom God chose to bring me into this world. Giving honor to our parents is especially important to God, so much so He has commanded us to do so.

Exodus 20:12 "Honor your father and your mother, that your days may be prolonged in the land which the Lord your God gives you." NASU

Glory to Your Name, O Lord! Thank You for the great honor and privilege it has been to be the youngest son of Betty Jones Williams, Your daughter and servant.

Should you take time to listen to *The Name of Jesus* you will hear in my voice a clearly discernible spirit of joy. This joy was springing forth from a renewed revelation of Jesus in my heart. I had been in a season wherein the Lord was enlarging my heart with momentary glimpses of His heart for every people, nation, tribe and tongue throughout the world. At first these heavenly glimpses so alarmed me to the condition of men's souls all I could think of was telling everyone I met of the impending danger and coming judgment. It was at this same time I wrote the song *Voices* (a passionate cry of my heart for the multitudes dying without Christ as their Savior) which became the title song to the project in which *The Name of Jesus* was included. There were days I would become so overwhelmed with the depravity and darkness of mankind I would begin to lose hope that what I was doing could ever make any difference against the seemingly overwhelming tide of wickedness. I desperately needed a renewed revelation of our mighty Conqueror and Savior Who came to destroy the deceiver of men's hearts. It's easier than one might realize to become overwhelmed at times with the onslaught of SIN and depravity all around us, especially if it's rampant in your own family and among your own children. However, just one look into the vastness of God's Redeeming Love instantaneously dispels all fear and concern replacing it with an unshakable confidence and hope in our victorious and soon coming King of kings and Lord of lords. By the grace of God, I SAW the Lord in the midst of the oncoming darkness, and immediately all my fears and doubts were swept away as I gazed upon the splendor of His majesty. Worthy are You, O Lord, to receive glory, honor, majesty and power. Glory to Your Name!

The Name of Jesus

(Song from the Voices project, music and lyrics written by Jerry Williams)

Glory and majesty be Yours
Honor and power forevermore
By Your Spirit and through Your Word
You've lifted Your Son over all the earth

Chorus:
Glory to Your Name!
The Name above all other names!

Glory to Your Name!
The Name of Jesus!

Through Your death and the blood You shed
You've given us wisdom and righteousness
You're our Hope, You're the Son of man
O worthy is the Lamb

Glory to Your Name!
The Name above all other names!
Glory to Your Name!
The Name of Jesus!

Glory to Your Name!
The Name above all other names!
Glory to Your Name!
The Name of Jesus!

DAY 17 JEAN ANN

I know your works, your labor, your patience, and that you cannot bear those who are evil. And you have tested those who say they are apostles and are not, and have found them liars; and you have persevered and have patience, and have labored for My name's sake and have not become weary. Nevertheless I have this against you, that you have left your first love. Revelation 2:2-4

It was September of 1963 and the beginning of a new school year. More importantly it was also my first year at Bowie Junior High School. I had just entered the seventh grade and it didn't take long to realize Junior High was an entirely different world than life had been at Pease Elementary. Things were bigger, harder and noticeably more fast-paced and exciting than elementary school ever was, but the biggest change that had unexpectedly happened in my life was GIRLS. Now that I was a big, bad Junior High student several of the new girls were suddenly sending me notes and purposefully walking past me in the lunch room. All the years I attended Pease Elementary this kind of behavior aggravated me to no end, but for some mysterious reason I wasn't being bothered at all by the attention these new girls were giving me now that I was in Junior High School. As a matter of fact, I actually found myself looking forward to it happening more and more. My mother had been teasing me all summer telling me how things would drastically change once I got to Junior High School. She kept saying, 'One of those pretty little girls is going to wink her eyes at you and the next thing you'll think is you're now in 'love'.' I, of course, told her she was crazy. That 'DAY' surprisingly came much sooner than I would have ever imagined. A few days after school had started I was walking through the hallway on my way to the cafeteria. Suddenly, I was stopped dead in my tracks by the sight of a 'girl'. (Although it's been nearly sixty years ago, I can still see her face in my mind's eye.) She was a dark-haired, brown-eyed 7th grader that I was seeing for the first time. That brief glance at a 'girl' in the hallway changed my life forever (some would say for the worse).

The next day when we passed each other again on our way to our next class she made a point to look right at me and say, 'Hi Jerry.' I must have turned forty shades of red. I had never blushed like that before, so I didn't exactly know how to act. I could hardly concentrate during my next class because all I could think about was the fact that the prettiest girl I had ever seen had spoken directly to me. After learning that her name was Jean Ann, it wasn't long before I mustered up the courage to actually say something back to her as we passed each other again in the hallway. Within a couple of weeks, she invited me to sit with her during lunch break. That was all it took. Cupid's arrows penetrated deep into my naïve heart and the gaff of 'first love' had me dangling like a fish doomed for that night's supper table. My mother's prophecy had come true. I was lock, stock and barrel smitten with 'young love'. For the next six months I proudly carried Jean Ann's books as I walked her to class. We met every day for lunch, and usually two or three times each week I would ride my bike over to her house after school to hang out for an hour or so. We were officially "going steady", even though I wasn't completely sure what that really meant. What I did know was that Jean Ann was now the center of my world and dominated my thoughts. I couldn't do anything or go anywhere without thinking about her and wanting to spend all my time with her. She was my "first love".

After a few weeks she began to drop hints that she really wanted our relationship to go somewhere we had never gone before and experience things we had never experienced together. What was this? I was great with the way things were. Why couldn't we just keep things like they had always been? But I knew something was going to have to change, and I knew I was the one who was going to have to take the responsibility to make the necessary changes happen. She was the one wanting more, and I knew exactly what that 'more' was. It was something I had never done before and the thought of how to do it honestly paralyzed me with fear. What would happen if I did it wrong? How do you do it right? As a result, I kept procrastinating and dodging what inevitably she desired to happen.

Finally, after six blissful months of expectation it happened...I kissed the beautiful Jean Ann. The inglorious event took place on her front porch after walking her home from school. Let me stop you right now and unequivocally tell you Hollywood has it all wrong. This wasn't one of those long drawn out lip locked marathons you so often see on the screen. It would be better described as something resembling a chicken violently pecking at their reflection in a window. But still...it was the FIRST KISS. What a relief! I had vanquished all fear and crossed over into the promised land. I had finally kissed the resplendent Jean Ann! As you would expect over the next several weeks we became more and more comfortable kissing each other. So much so that without even realizing it things began to slowly change for reasons neither of us understood. Over time the wondrous mystery, expectation and joy of that first kiss became muddled and forgotten by what seemed like a thousand other experimental kisses. Embracing the beautiful Jean Ann had now become more of an expected duty and routine which ushered in a slow and deadly change in our relationship. Now it was almost like we had begun to analyze how we kissed each other rather than simply enjoying being together. It wasn't long after this point we both acknowledged we had mutually lost that mysteriously wonderful feeling we had at first and should probably 'break up'. I had never 'broken up' with anyone before, so I didn't know if I was supposed to be sad and mope around for a few days or what. After the 'break up' it hit me, I had spent most of the last year spending the bulk of my free time with Jean Ann, talking with her every night, walking her to class, eating lunch with her every day, talking about her to all the guys and seeing her in the stands wearing my varsity jacket during the games. Now that she was no longer in my life what was I supposed to do now? That's when Lynette, her best friend, stepped in to fill the void. It didn't take long before I was thinking Jean Ann who?

I shared this story of the innocence and delight of my 'first love' because it so perfectly parallels the journey most of us have experienced in our relationship with the Lord. Every truly born again believer I know, if they are really honest, would admit that when they first came to personally know the Lord they were exhilarated by the love, mercy, grace, hope, forgiveness and acceptance they felt when in His presence. Remember how in those early days the Lord was all you could think about and the One you wanted to be with all the time? It didn't matter where you went or what you were doing, Jesus was the center of your world continuously dominating all your thoughts, words and actions. Can you recall how amazing it was when He did impossible things for you that you never expected? Oh, what blissful times in His presence that always left you wondering whether you should laugh, cry, shout or just sit at His feet and tell Him how much you loved and thanked Him for being there. Now, can you also remember when things began to slowly 'cool down' and that spontaneous conscious life you had with Him began evolving into more of a systematic, predictable relationship wherein everything you did was analyzed and graded by you and others for approval? Remember? That's when things started becoming 'routine' in your relationship with the Lord. It wasn't long after that the mysteriously wonderful consciousness of His presence faded and all that remained was the 'routine'. One can only 'go through the motions' so long before you start losing interest in spending time maintaining a 'routine' for appearances. That's when you begin exploring and searching for other avenues to fill the void left from losing your 'first love'. In the end all you've really done is 'broken up' in your heart with your 'FIRST LOVE' and moved on to Lynette.

The great news for all of us who have had those seasons wherein we've struggled in our devotion and love for God is this: He never wavers in His love for us. He loves us unconditionally. His love for us never loses its power, passion or purpose. He is fully aware of our tendencies to wander and waffle in our devotion to Him, but still has forgiven and accepted us to be His Bride throughout all eternity. He is not taken back by our seasons of 'coolness' toward Him, but is fully able to 'revive' our hearts when we return to Him as our 'first love'.

Jesus said to him, You shall love the LORD your God with all your heart, with all your soul, and with all your mind. This is the first and great commandment. And the second is like it: You shall love your neighbor as yourself. On these two commandments hang all the Law and the Prophets. Matthew 22:37-40

<u>Prayer</u>

Dear Heavenly Father,

You are the essence, the Author and the embodiment of Perfect, Pure Love. May Your love continually consume and control the motives and motions of my heart. Then will my work, words and wishes be pleasing to You and beneficial to others. Without Your love as the foundation of my life all I endeavor to do will account for nothing. When wholly submitted to Your love I will cease seeking my own promotion, cease being envious of the advancements of others and cease any conversation that is unkind, disrespectful of others or coarse in its content. With Your love as my Source and daily sustenance I will rejoice in the Truth, believe in the unbelievable, hope for the hopeless, bear with the failures and flaws of others and joyfully endure whatever difficulties come my way. Help me, Father, to never again wander from that which I cannot live without - Your Love. I love You, O my God and Redeemer. Amen.

(Lyrics from 'Burn Me With Your Love' – Voices CD)

In the presence of the Lord
Is an all-consuming fire
That tests the plan and purpose
Of each man and of each heart.
Many who are wise,
When they come before His eyes
Are cast upon the rocks of ruined men.

So, burn me with Your love,
Burn me with Your love!
Take away the wooden treasures
I've gathered from this world!
Burn me with Your love,
Burn me with Your love
That I might stand before You
As Your son!

<u>The Story Behind the Song:</u>

As you read through the lyrics of *In the Early Days* it will be obvious why I specifically chose this song for this devotional. At the very least it's an embarrassment how many times through the years I have bartered my dreams and affections on the open market to see who or what might offer me some new and fresh experience or feeling. In every instance I ended up bankrupt emotionally and spiritually. Mercifully God has always been there to rescue me from my own ignorance and pride. The following lyrics will take you on a scenic ride through the mountains and valleys I blindly wandered into eventually becoming imprisoned by the momentary glitter of worldly approval. In the first four lines you will see the mountain of 'glory' I encountered. In the early days I never considered receiving 'glory' for anything I did knowing it was God Who did ALL things through me. Then came the years where I had #1 songs on the radio, thousands coming to the concerts, tens of thousands purchasing my music, etc. Slowly, but certainly, I began to take credit for some of the 'glory' that alone belongs to the Lord. Deadly mistake! The next few lines address the prominence of prayer in my life. How much you truly love someone is directly related to how much you pray for them. When God was my first and ONLY LOVE, I prayed to Him continually. Ever so slowly that part of my life was consumed with other 'more pressing' things that had to be done to keep the ministry moving forward. Another Deadly mistake! The last few lines deal with tolerating sin in my life by allowing possessions to begin possessing my heart. Yet again, a Deadly mistake! Through it all the Lord never left or forsook me, but He lovingly and mercifully stripped me of everything that so easily hindered my life and walk with Him. Today He is once again the supreme LOVE of my life, my DREAM come true, my closest FRIEND and my greatest desire. I love You, Lord. You are my HOPE and my FUTURE!

In the Early Days
(Song from the Mighty River project, music and lyrics written by Jerry Williams)

In the early days I had a dream to be holy
And conquer the nations through love
In the early days I'd never share in the glory
Or praises of men's applause

In the early days I never thought it a problem

To pray every night for all men
In the early days in my heart nothing mattered
More than to be with Him

Chorus: Oh-h Jesus, I want to go back
To the days of my first love!
Oh-h Jesus, take me back
In my heart to my first love!

In the early days I can remember the battles
I'd fight every night with my sin
In the early days I can remember how often
I'd fall on my knees and repent

In the early days I often gave my possessions
To people who had less than me
In the early days I was completely abandoned
To living my life for Him!

Chorus

In the early days I would tell people whenever
I met them that they should repent
And in the early days I would get angry whenever
The devil hurt one of my friends

In the early days singing songs unto Jesus
Never became a routine
In the early days I wanted only to please Him
Through faith that could do anything!

Chorus

Tag: Take me back, take me back,
Take me back to my first love! (2x's)

DAY 18 A GLIMPSE OF HEAVEN

For this corruptible must put on incorruption, and this mortal must put on immortality. So when this corruptible has put on incorruption, and this mortal has put on immortality, then shall be brought to pass the saying that is written: Death is swallowed up in victory. O Death, where is your sting? O Hades, where is your victory? 1 Corinthians 15:53-55 NKJV

On several occasions I have been called to the bedsides of those who were on the threshold of physical death to pray, comfort, encourage, console and at times even confront them concerning their faith in their final moments in this realm. The following story relates two such occasions which remarkably occurred with the same person, Betty Williams, who was my mother and one of the great heroines of faith, hope and love I have ever known. The first call came early on a Sunday morning in the spring of 1982. At the time I was in Evansville, Indiana where I had been invited to minister at a large Assembly of God church in the city. Our team had already ministered to the youth during Sunday School when I unexpectedly received word from a family member that 'Granny' had been rushed to the hospital and was dying with lung cancer. As I reached for the phone the words I heard were: 'They're going to try and get her stabilized overnight, then do radical lung surgery on her tomorrow. The doctors have been very direct with us and do not expect she will survive the surgery. You've got to come immediately!' I turned and relayed the news to the leadership of the church, then within only a few moments was loaded and on my way to Odessa, Texas. I calculated it would take approximately fourteen hours to make the drive which meant I would arrive between 1:00 and 2:00 a.m. if I drove straight through. However, I was already extremely tired from the ministry schedule we had been keeping for the last several weeks, and I also had my young family on the road with me. Therefore, I determined that driving all night was unwise and decided to stop for a few hours so we could get some much needed sleep. As we made our way toward Odessa I prayed continuously standing on the promise God had given me in 1971 that my mother would not die until she had given her heart to Jesus. Outwardly she was a hard-working, hard living independent woman who wouldn't think twice about giving you a piece of her mind. She often came across as someone angry and bitter toward the Lord and made it perfectly clear she didn't want anything to do with church or any other religious nonsense. Not long after I had committed my life to Christ she literally screamed in my face saying, 'I'm going to hell! So, leave me alone and let me enjoy it!' From that day on I had been continually pleading with the Lord for her salvation, and He had promised me she would one day be gloriously saved.

One of the most deadly and effective weapons the enemy uses against us when we are attempting to stand in faith for a supernatural healing are the brutal reports you continuously hear from the doctors. I understand they are obligated to tell you all the worst case scenarios, but it's almost always in direct opposition to what the Lord is speaking to your heart. So, while driving the long trek to West Texas I had to fight against all the reports we were receiving suggesting she might die before we ever arrived there. By the grace of God, the longer I drove the stronger my confidence grew that she would not die before calling on Jesus to save her. This newly energized confidence in His promise kept me keenly focused as we made our way westward. At some point during the long drive the Holy Spirit powerfully implanted within my heart a clear 'word' concerning what I was to do when I arrived at the hospital. This 'word' was so dominating my spirit by the time I drove into the parking lot of the Medical Center I was filled with a bold expectation and excitement confident God was about to do something miraculous and impossible. It's hard to explain, but there are times in your life as a believer when you just 'know' God is with you and about to do the miraculous. This was one of those times. We arrived four hours before Granny was scheduled to go in for surgery (the surgery the doctors said she would not survive).

As I quickly made my way to her room, much to my surprise there were five nurses already in the room preparing to transport her to surgery. Unexpectedly the doctor had moved the time of the surgery up four hours. By the grace of God we had made it just in time. This, of course, was not a coincidence, but God moving heaven and earth to fulfill His Word. Usually I would have stayed out of the way and let the staff do their job, but not this time. Instead, I boldly walked into the room and under the anointing of the Holy Spirit proclaimed to the five nurses, 'I need all of you to leave the room for a few moments, please.' They all looked at me in wonderment and without saying a word quietly departed leaving me in the room alone with my nearly deceased mother. I then looked into my mother's fading eyes and confidently told her the Lord had sent me there as His ambassador of Life. I said, 'Mom, don't be afraid. The Lord has assured me you will not die, but will live many more years for His glory'. She began to cry tears of hope. Suddenly a dark, smothering presence filled the room making it hard to even normally breathe. A gloom began falling over my mother instantly robbing her of any hope and she began to slip away. In that moment I knew I was an eye witness of the dark side of eternity, something every person should experience at least once in their lives. Without hesitation I raised my voice and loudly proclaimed what the Lord had directed me to say, 'In the name of Jesus I rebuke you, spirit of death. You have no authority, power or jurisdiction in this place or over this woman. She belongs to God and I command you to leave immediately!' In an instant the ominous spirit of death was vanquished by the blood of the Lamb and my mother began to smile again. I prayed with her, then confidently called for the nurses to take her away. Not only did she NOT DIE in the surgery, but she made it through in record time. Then, for the next twenty years she baffled the doctors shattering every medical record for those who had gone through the same radical surgical procedure. Hallelujah!

Soon after Granny was able to leave the hospital we moved her to our new ministry headquarters which was now located in East Texas. The first thing I did after we got her situated in East Texas was give her a new Bible which she would read when no one was looking. I can't say exactly when, but sometime during the nine months of recuperating and daily reading her Bible she was radically transformed in her heart. Granny was gloriously saved as the living Word of God took root in her heart and opened her eyes to the Hope that is found only in Jesus. She eventually joined our ministry staff and for nearly a decade ministered to thousands of people all across this world. Hallelujah.

The second time I had the honor of being at Granny's bedside as she was again on the doorstep of physical death was twenty years later in February of 2002. The story leading up to my being at her bedside actually began two weeks earlier. By this time Granny was living in Waynesboro, PA with my sister and we had relocated to a suburb of Houston, TX. Early one morning as I was spending time with the Lord suddenly the presence of God consciously filled the room. I literally began to rejoice and weep at the same time. As I often do I picked up my old guitar and began worshipping the Lord. The Holy Spirit instantly began pouring into my spirit a new song out of the scripture I was presently reading. Within just a few moments He had given me a powerful new song which I entitled *The Angels Anthem*. Then I clearly heard Him say, 'This song is for your mother and I have given it to you to sing over her.' It was only three days later when I received a call from my sister saying that Granny had taken a dramatic turn for the worse and was physically plummeting. I caught the first available flight out of Houston to Baltimore, then drove straight to the hospital in Chambersburg, PA which was approximately 100 miles to the West. When I arrived I was greeted by several family members who had all gathered to be with Granny. We all hugged and then my precious sister encouraged everyone to allow me to be with Granny alone. As soon as they had all exited the room I pulled a chair up as close as possible to Granny's bedside and began telling her many things the Lord had spoken to my heart during the flight concerning her victorious life. I honored her legacy and proclaimed His unwavering love for her, His daughter. Unlike the time before in 1982, this time I shared with my amazing mother that God had sent me there to prepare her for her glorious graduation.

At that time, I stood up leaning over her bed and said, 'Mom, the Lord has given me a song to sing over you tonight to prepare your heart for what you are about to see. In a few moments you will see Jesus, the Risen Lamb of God, sitting at the right hand of Almighty God, and all the host of heaven crying out, 'Worthy is the Lamb'! Mom, in a few moments you, too, will be singing this song to the Lord.' Then I gently leaned even closer to her and began singing *The Angels' Anthem*, the very song I had received only four days earlier. God's presence again filled the room, but this time it was even stronger. There was something incredibly wonderful about this manifestation of His glorious presence. There was joy, peace, love, hope and expectation overwhelming every fiber of our being. It was exhilarating, but I was well aware I was an honored guest at a heavenly coronation God had prepared for His precious daughter. As soon as I finished singing His song to His daughter, I then proclaimed the following scripture He had directed me to speak over her at that precise moment:

And now I commend you to God, and to the Word of His grace which is able to build you up and give you the inheritance among all those who are sanctified. Acts 20:32

Within less than sixty seconds after speaking that scripture over Granny, the Lord translated her spirit home to be with Him forever. This time there was no warfare or spirit of death, only the sweet aroma of God's presence and a peace that was not of this world. I was overwhelmed with a sense of honor as I sat quietly in the room with what I knew was a true hero of the faith. This time was her predetermined time with Him set aside by God Himself before time ever began. This was truly one of the greatest moments and most cherished honors of my life.

As you read the words and possibly take time to listen to *The Angel's Anthem* it is my hope you will each be encouraged and strengthened in your hope and confidence for the days ahead. May the eyes of your heart be opened to see, if only for a moment, a glimpse of heaven. Then you will in part know how powerful the experience was for me as an earthly son, a child of God and a minister. I truly believe death for the believer is never a tragic event, but is in fact a graduation with honors. See you soon, Mom!

Prayer

Dear Father,
I wholly acknowledge and proclaim You alone are the Giver and the Keeper of Life. I further acknowledge my inability to fully comprehend the magnitude of all You have made possible for me, an unworthy and undeserving benefactor of Your Life. Thank You for choosing, delivering and redeeming my soul from certain death. Thank You for loving me while I was yet a sinner. Thank You for sending Your only Son, Jesus Christ, to rescue and redeem my perishing soul. With this immeasurable bounty of goodness and heavenly favor, how is it possible I still wrestle with daily fears and temptations? Oh my merciful Father, deliver me from any

remaining fear of the unknown, the fear that grips most men in the face of death. Help me to see with the eyes of faith that glorious place You are preparing for all Your children beyond the veil of this momentary existence. Keep me from living my life as though I will never depart this momentary realm, but help me to live in such a way as to prove I am a sojourner in this place and a citizen of heaven. Take from me every fleshly, ungodly desire for the securities of this world that my hope might wholly rest in the certainty of Your life in me. May all the remaining days of my time on earth be filled with endeavors that bring me and many others closer to You. I long to be forever united with You in that place where nothing defiles, and where there is no grief, sorrow, separation, sin, fear, failure, pain or death. Until then, may I be faithful in my preparation and ever joyful in my expectation of one day soon casting every crown of accomplishment and honor I may gain here at Your feet. Worthy is the Lamb Who was slain! My Redeemer lives! Amen.

I take, O cross thy shadow, For my abiding place
I ask no other sunshine than the sunshine of His face
Content to let the world go by, to know no gain or loss
My sinful self my only shame, My glory all the cross!

The Story Behind the Song:

Even though I've written thousands of songs in my life, there are a few that will forever dwell in the secret chamber of my heart because of their importance in my life personally. *The Angels Anthem* is one of those rare and special songs. The Lord gave me this song in January of 2002 as I was sitting in my garage in La Porte, TX spending time worshipping the Lord. Each morning I would open the garage door, sit in my old rocking chair with my Bible in hand, then sing, pray and shout to the Lord. I always had one of my old guitars close by just in case the Lord blessed me with a new song. On a crisp January morning in 2002 as I was reading in Revelation imagining the spectacular scene that surrounds the throne of God, suddenly the presence of God overwhelmed the entire space. All I could do was cry out, 'Worthy is the Lamb! Worthy is the Lamb!' I was instantaneously filled with a powerful revelation of Jesus sitting at the right hand of the Throne of God. The presence of God was so prevalent all I could do was cry tears of joy and sit in wonderment. Within moments I picked up my old guitar and began writing *The Angels Anthem* in response to the amazing revelation I had just received from the Lord. Then I heard the Lord clearly speak to my heart saying, 'I am giving you this song for your mother'. A few days later we received a call from my sister telling me that Granny had taken a sudden turn for the worse and I needed to come immediately. I caught a flight out the next day and arrived in Pennsylvania that evening. As I entered her hospital room in Chambersburg, PA the rest of the family gave me their greetings, then graciously left the room so I could spend some time alone with my mother. For the first several minutes I shared with her how grateful I was that God had chosen me to be her son, and how blessed my life was because of her sacrifices and love for me throughout all the years. Then, following the urging of the Holy Spirit, I leaned forward and said, 'Mom, the Lord has given me a song He wants me to sing over you right now'. I stood as one would stand when honoring a dignitary, then leaned as close to her as possible and sang *The Angels Anthem* over her. The fact I was able to do this without bursting into tears was a miracle in itself. As I sang, once again the presence of God filled the room and a peace that passes all understanding was prominent. Within less than sixty seconds after finishing the song the Lord called His daughter home with Him for all eternity. It was literally one of the most beautiful moments I have ever experienced in the presence of the Lord, and one of the most treasured gifts I have ever been given by the Lord for someone else. I sincerely pray as you read through the lyrics of this special song you will be translated in your spirit to the very throne room of God wherein all anxiety, fear, worry and doubt will be replaced with that peace and confidence in Christ that keeps us until the day we will see Him face to face.

The Angels Anthem

(Title song from The Angels Anthem project, music and lyrics written by Jerry Williams)

As I raised my heart toward heaven
I could hear the angels all around the Throne singing "Worthy"
Then I saw the Living Creatures falling down before the presence
Of the One Who is "Worthy"
Then the elders threw their crowns before the Risen Lamb
And the host of heaven raised their voice in praise singing

Chorus
Worthy is the Lamb Who was slain!
Worthy is the Lamb now He ever reigns!
Worthy is, worthy is, worthy is the Lamb!

Then I turned my eyes and suddenly
I saw the One Who sits upon the Throne Who is "Worthy"
And there is nothing to describe
What I saw or what I felt within my heart for He is "Holy"
Then I bowed and gave the glory to the Risen Lamb
And all of heaven raised their voice in praise singing

Chorus x 2

DAY 19 ALL MEN ARE LIKE GRASS

All flesh is grass, and all its loveliness is like the flower of the field. The grass withers, the flower fades, because the breath of the LORD blows upon it. Surely the people are grass. The grass withers, the flower fades, but the word of our God stands forever.
Isaiah 40:6-8 NKJV

In January of 2007 the Lord made it clear to us it was time to quit living full time on our motor coach and 'put down roots' for the future. This was a significant 'word' for us since in obedience to the Holy Spirit's leading in 2002 we had sold our home, purchased a 40-foot-long motor coach, liquidated or gave away nearly all our worldly possessions, and had been crisscrossing the states freely ministering to those leaders to whom the Lord directed us to go. After much prayer we took a step of faith and established a home base in Texarkana, TX. By design this newly acquired home was established as a Leadership Resource and Dream Center (LRDC). Our plan was to create a prototype model LRDC that could be reproduced in other regions of the country as the ministry grew. Establishing each LRDC in a home environment greatly helps in breaking down long standing barriers we often face when counseling isolated, betrayed, wounded and hurting leaders. The LRDC in the Texarkana area was a beautiful home on two acres just outside the city limits in Beaver Lake Estates. Although the home itself needed very little work inside, the large yard was nothing more than a series of spotty weed patches with a few areas of native grass sparsely scattered about. On the north side adjacent to the property was an undeveloped three-acre plot of land drastically overgrown with weeds, large amounts of nettle vines and wild grasses. Since our purpose for each LRDC is to offer a place of rest, hope, restoration and practical resource for leaders, I needed to do something immediately about the scraggly looking yard. In truth this was a project that was actually appealing to me since I love working outside in the yard. My love for yardwork began when I was just a little boy. Believe it or not when I was only six years old I could be seen pushing our little red lawn mower up and down the neighborhood streets knocking on doors of homes that needed their lawns mowed. I would mow and hand trim any yard (front and back) for five dollars (three dollars if you didn't want it trimmed). I'm sure it was quite a shock for the neighbors when they opened their front door only to be confronted by a six-year-old asking if they wanted their yard mowed.

During our more than sixty months living full time on the motor coach I would always offer to mow the property, as well as clean up and improve the landscaping around the churches and ministry homes where we were invited to minister. This often gave me wonderful opportunities to use many of the practical things I've learned about landscaping to personally minister to the leadership of the church. One of those practical lessons I've used over and over is this: Never let things 'go to seed'. I learned at an early age if you consistently keep mowing the grass and weeds together not allowing either of them to 'go to seed', eventually the grass will mysteriously begin spreading out like a carpet ultimately taking full possession of the yard. As I stared at the nearly two-acre yard in Beaver Lake Estates I quickly determined this would once again be my time proven singular strategy for the pitiful looking yard. Week after week I faithfully mowed the scraggly growth until surprisingly, in less than six months the transformation was almost complete. The large weed patch that was the front yard (approximately one acre) was now a lush, green lawn. In less than a year neighbors began stopping by and inquiring how I was able to get the yard to look so beautiful so quickly. My answer was always the same, 'Never let it GO TO SEED'.

What a great lesson to learn not only for your lawn, but also for your life: NEVER LET THINGS GO TO SEED. As I pondered the opening verses to this devotional (Isaiah 40:6-8) I was instantly translated back to 1976 when I was living in Orlando, FL and serving on the pastoral staff of a local church. The majority of the mowing that was going on in my life that year was the Holy Spirit continuously cutting down the ugly, scraggly weeds that kept popping up in my heart. For thirteen long months the Holy Spirit continuously worked on the ugly pride and arrogant attitudes that were trying to take over my thoughts and actions. Oftentimes all you would see was a cloud of dust being stirred up as He faithfully mowed the soil of my life. Slowly things began to change as the landscape of my heart became more and more something people wanted to stop and look at. Eventually I grew to love the nurturing and mowing of the Holy Spirit in my heart understanding that Him never allowing me to 'GO TO SEED' He was actually increasing the lush, beautiful landscape of Christ in me while decreasing the ugly weeds of my scraggly flesh. To God be all the glory and praise.

It's amazing to me how many today want all the blessings, but are unwilling to submit to the only process that will keep them from 'going to seed'. I realize how truly blessed I have been seeing, hearing and experiencing countless things millions of believers still only dream about. All the experiences and encounters I have had throughout the years have led me to be more convinced than ever that were it not for the continual disciplining (mowing) of the Lord in my life there would be little or nothing praiseworthy or beautiful to see in me today. I have learned (just like I did mowing yards as a little boy) that this holy process of mowing and landscaping the soil of my heart is absolutely necessary to maintain Christ in me as the beautiful and resplendent covering of my life. My heavenly Father is the Great Gardener of my soul and He will never allow the weeds to overcome and conquer the soil of my heart. His disciplines are a response of His love and purpose for me. That is precisely why, to the glory of God, every weed patch I presently have attempting to take root in my heart or mind is being steadily choked out through the continual mowing the Holy Spirit is doing in me. The Great Landscaper of my eternal soul has begun a good work in me and HE WILL not remove His Hands from the soil of my life until that WORK is complete in Christ. Hallelujah!

I don't want to 'mow' you down with this thought, but let me make one last point. In real estate there is a phrase that is often used concerning one's property and yard. That phrase is: CURB APPEAL. When Donna and I purchased our first home in an older neighborhood of La Porte, Texas, it was one of the newest (nine years old) and smallest houses on the street. It had been built for an elderly lady who subsequently never did anything inside or outside during the nine years she owned the property. Needless to say the place was a 'curb appeal' mess which caused the price to drastically drop allowing us to get a phenomenal 'deal'. We spent the next three years painstakingly working inside and outside the house radically transforming its 'curb appeal'. When the Lord told us it was time to move, remarkably the house sold the very day it was listed. One of the primary reasons it sold to the first person who looked at it was the beautiful yard and the wonderful feeling everyone got when entering inside. People would come over and sit outside just to enjoy the gardens filled with roses and other flowers that were prospering from their continual care and pruning. In other words, the CURB APPEAL sold the house. That thought makes me wonder if we were to get an unbiased quote on the current 'curb appeal' of our lives, how we would rate? It is my desire that whoever encounters my life sees the Lord and His handiwork on display. He is the Lily of the Valley and the Rose of Sharon. I want to be a reflection of His beauty in the earth so that all who see me will ask, 'How did you get your yard looking so good'? I will simply tell them the Great Landscaper and Gardener of my soul kept the weeds and grass continuously mowed thereby never letting anything in my heart 'go to seed'.

Prayer

Dear Father,

You Who are the ever faithful Gardener and Vinedresser of my heart, thank You for Your continual pruning in my life. Thank You for not leaving me to wildly grow and thereby live in imminent danger of 'going to seed'. Like David I proclaim, 'Before I was afflicted I went astray, but now I keep Your word'. Even though it is painful when I am being necessarily pruned, I know it is for my good and Your glory. Oh, how I long for Your righteousness and holiness to become the ever present 'curb appeal' of my life. I know this is not possible unless I yield to Your 'mowing' the wild grasses and weeds of wickedness in my heart and soul. I am Yours, O Lord! Do whatever is needful to keep me from 'going to seed'! Cultivate me as You will and may the good seed of heaven grow mightily in the soil of my life. Amen.

The Story Behind the Song:

I wrote *Seed of Faith* during the early years God called, anointed and released me to be a forerunner of contemporary Christian music (CCM). In those early days we were Spirit led trailblazers for what has become today a world-wide platform for music. I can assure you it wasn't that way in the beginning. There were no existing tried and tested models to follow, no video networks to launch a career, no internet, no YouTube, and precious few ministers who would support the use of guitars and drums in the sanctuary. Consequently, every day was a step of faith and every song we wrote and recorded was an open book that chronicled our struggles and hopes through the journey. Those were great days as we daily depended on the Lord to take what was seemingly unusable and turn it into a beautiful garden in which multitudes would find peace, comfort, joy and strength. We had no idea God would 'do' all He did through our feeble efforts to follow Him in those days. He continually corrected (mowed) and remolded (landscaped) us as we made a thousand mistakes along the way. Still, the *Seed of Faith* that had been planted by our simple obedience became a mighty tree under which many have taken refuge throughout the years. To God be all the glory.

In each of you there is a similar *Seed of Faith*. The choice is yours to leave it there untouched, or to take a step of faith and plant the seed in the soil of obedience and believe God to do something through you no one else believes is possible. That's right! It's a miracle waiting to happen in and through your life, but the seed has to be planted to grow. What are you waiting on? Dig a hole and plant the seed. The possibilities are out of this world!

Seed of Faith
(Song from the 'It's All right Now' project, music and lyrics written by Jerry Williams)

Jesus You said if I'd believe in You
I could do the same things that You did
You said all it takes is a seed of faith
And my mountains would fall in the sea

My battles are won and the lost they would come
And give their hearts to You as their King
Oh, Lord I can't wait to use my seed of faith
And see the miracle begin in me

Jesus You promised You would help me be strong
If I came to You every day
When I'm at work or when I'm at home
I'd talk about the things that You said

So claiming Your word I'm gonna be heard
I'm gonna tell everybody I see
That Jesus is Lord and the battle is won

And the miracle's alive in me
Chorus:
Listen My son I want you to grow
But there's too many reasons you should make it slow
If you make it too fast you'll wither like the grass
When the heat of a trial comes your way
Slow yourself down and sit at My feet
Don't get in a hurry or you'll suffer defeat
Be still and know that I am the Lord
And you'll stand forevermore

Lord, You said that it's those who are led
By You Spirit who are called Your sons
You said if I'm alive in You then I'm dead
To the pressures that so often come

They try to tear me down so I'd lose what I've found
Life and peace in You
Oh, I'm gonna stand and be a mighty man
No matter what the devil may do

Chorus

DAY 20 BE CAREFUL WHAT YOU ASK FOR

Let no one deceive you with empty words.. Ephesians 5:6

It was early 1974 and we were settling into what would be our new home for the next year, a small, older two-bedroom ground floor apartment in Kissimmee, Florida. I'll never forget that place primarily because of the overpowering smell of rotten eggs that came from the Sulphur content in the water. We moved there because of the low cost and its proximity to a family who were on the board of our ministry at that time. Also, it was only fifteen minutes away from the small Baptist Church where I had just become the new (and first) full time associate/youth pastor. I took the position at the church so I could be home more and start a family. My starting salary was only $750.00 per month which meant we had to be very careful with our money each month. Even though the salary was well below normal, I knew this was where the Lord was leading us, so I took the position and trusted the Lord to supply in other ways. Our little apartment was only two blocks from West Lake Toho which was one of the premier fishing lakes in the state. Consequently, once we were settled in I decided to take up fishing strictly as a potential resource to help supplement our food each week. Getting started presented a number of challenges since I was born and raised in the oil fields of West Texas where there were sand dunes, snakes, multiple varieties of cactus, mesquite trees, horned toads, lizards, tarantulas, and you guessed it, no nearby lakes. Thankfully I did own a fishing rod, but it was the same rod and reel combo I had been given by my step dad when I was just a kid. I still have no idea how I ended up with that old rod and reel, but when I finally pulled it out of storage I'm fairly confident it still had the original line on it. Not exactly the best start to a successful and bountiful fishing career. Still, none of those things dampened my resolve to learn how to fish, and eventually help feed my family in the process. My first strategic step was to talk with everyone in the church who had a reputation for being good at 'fishing'. Then, I started reading whatever articles I could get my hands on concerning fresh water fishing in Florida. It wasn't long before I began taking what I was learning straight to the lake to practice. After all, practice makes perfect, right? For the first few weeks all I could do was stand on the bank and cast. That soon moved into 'wade fishing' which I had seen a few guys doing. The more I studied and practiced the better I became, even though my equipment was drastically out of date. Still, I had no way of getting to those areas of the lake where the majority of the fish congregated and where most of the 'fish stories' were coming from. Eventually all the hard work began paying off as I started catching a few fish on a regular basis, and actually began putting food on our table at least one day each week. Then I got my biggest opportunity as a couple of men from the church who owned bass boats invited me to go out with them. What a difference it was going to their 'honey holes', none of which could be reached without a boat. Every time I was invited to go out on their boat we would always come home with more fish than I wanted to clean (they always gave me their fish).

The climax of my first year learning how to fish in Florida came when it became possible for me to acquire a small 14-foot fiberglass boat from an elderly gentleman who no longer had the strength or desire to go fishing. It was a modest V-hull boat nothing like the bass rigs others had. None of that mattered to me, though. I still felt like the captain of an ocean liner that first afternoon I headed out for my maiden voyage. I double and triple checked everything I could think of, then took off for the nearest boat launch on West Lake Toho. Chuck Hughes, my fishing mentor and one of the men of our church, had graciously equipped me with new line for my old open face Garcia reel, and also gave me a tackle box he no longer used that included several artificial baits. Thanks to Chuck the six-inch black plastic worms with the appropriate hooks and slip weights had become my favorite bait to use. I cautiously, but proudly launched my craft, then with tremendous expectation started up the anemic sounding 9.5 hp Evinrude motor.

I slowly made my way out onto the lake and headed directly for a large patch of hyacinth (a hot bed for big bass, something I learned from Chuck while taking me fishing in his boat). I began quietly drifting through the hyacinth carefully doing everything Chuck had taught me when suddenly I felt a bump on the end of my line. I gently lowered the broken tip of that old Garcia pole and made a perfect hook set on the unaware fish. As soon as I set the hook the fish took off like a raging bull trying to throw its unwelcome rider. My old Garcia spin cast reel began to sing as the powerful fish began pulling several yards of the new line out. For the first time in years that old pole was bent in half and all I could do was hang on and pray the line (or the pole) didn't break. Within a few seconds the fish turned and I started working him back toward the boat. I must have cried out, 'Jesus! Jesus! Help me Lord,' ten times before I got the fish through all the hyacinth and close to the boat. The whole time I was fighting the monster I had it in my mind I was about to land my first Florida trophy bass. Then suddenly it broke the surface and I saw it! Wow! Was it big! It was by far the biggest fish I had ever hooked. Hallelujah! Praise the Lord! Then, as the monster broke the surface again my exuberance turned to wonderment. Within a couple of minutes, the big fish was landed and at first I just sat there staring at the trophy. I knew what catfish, gar, carp and bass looked like, but I had no idea what I was gazing at flopping in the bottom of my boat. After a couple of minutes, I shook off my disappointment that it wasn't a trophy bass and basked in the ecstasy of having caught the largest fish of my life. Nothing else mattered. This was a huge fish and I was not only going to figure out what it was, but also how to clean it and somehow get it onto my table for a victorious conqueror's meal. I fished a few more minutes, but my thoughts were now fully dominated by my prize fish, so I decided to quickly pack up and head back to the boat ramp.

As I share the rest of the story keep in mind that even though I now owned a boat and everything else that made me look like a seasoned fisherman, I was still a novice who needed older, wiser fishermen to mold, teach and guide me.

Approaching the boat ramp, I noticed an old, seasoned fisherman sitting in the back of his boat still tied up to the docking area. He was quite a sight as he sat shirtless in his dock shoes (no socks), shorts, and Bing Crosby hat staring at the sunset while holding an opened can of beer in his right hand. His skin looked like weathered, worn out tree bark and was surprisingly almost the same color as the monster fish I had just victoriously landed. My first thought seeing him was, 'I don't think there's a mosquito within fifty miles that could successfully penetrate this old guy's reptilian skin'. Then in an instant I had what I was certain was an epiphany, 'If there's anyone who knows what I've caught and what to do with it, then it has to be this guy, right?' I expectantly and slowly pulled up next to him in my sturdy craft then politely said, 'Excuse me, sir. I'm sorry to bother you, but I'm from Texas and recently moved here with my family. I am a newcomer to fishing and just caught a big fish I have never seen before. Can you please tell me what kind of fish it is (I held up the large fish with pride) and whether or not it's any good to eat?'

Forgive me for pausing again, but before I go on with the rest of the story, you need to understand those same mosquitoes that couldn't hope to penetrate the old man's buzzard like skin were beginning to bombard me as though I were the early bird special. Within less than ten minutes I was literally being devoured by the little demons while trying to patiently wait for this old fisherman to impart some vital knowledge and much needed wisdom.

While I sat there continuously swatting mosquitos the shirtless old fisherman never moved a single muscle other than his mouth. The entire time he spoke, he did so sitting perfectly motionless except for when he would slightly raise his eyes just high enough to make sure he still had my full attention. After momentarily glancing at the monster fish, he replied, 'Oh, yeah! You've caught a big ole mud fish.' I quickly asked, 'Are these fish any good to eat?' He never said yes, but instead began to expound in great detail exactly how to clean and prepare the fish for supper later that night. He painstakingly shared the precise ingredients I needed to purchase and how to blend them together to make his favorite basting solution. Wow! I kept thinking I had hit the jackpot because this old guy knew everything I needed to learn about cleaning and cooking my prize fish. On and on he went educating me on the basics of how to clean and prepare 'mud fish'.

Then, thankfully at some point just before it turned dark he said, 'After you've done all these steps, then find a clean board and carefully attach each filet to the board. After basting the fillets, then place bacon strips over them and liberally baste them one last time.' By this time I felt like I had lost about a pint of blood, but it didn't matter since I was learning how to clean and cook Florida 'mud fish' for the first time. His last directions to me were, (Remember he never moved during the whole conversation), 'Finally place the board in the oven at 350 degrees and cook it for fifteen or twenty minutes, or until the bacon is crisp on top. When you've done all that, then take the board out of the oven, throw away the fish and EAT THE BOARD!' For about ten seconds I sat glaring in unbelief at the leather-skinned old fisherman. Without saying another word, I gently slipped the mud fish off the stringer back into the now dark water (amazingly it was still very much alive), then quickly loaded my little boat. Before I pulled away I took one last glance at the old codger who had just taken me for a wild ride at my blood letting expense and his great pleasure. Had I not felt so stupid I am sure I would have laughed as I do these days about the entire encounter. On that day I was the 'big fish' that got hooked, landed, filleted and laid out on a platter ready for the serving.

Mercifully I not only survived the embarrassment of that encounter with the old fisherman, but used it as motivation to work even harder to become a competent fisherman. Within a couple of years I had become so proficient as a fisherman we started having fish fry's at the church feeding dozens of families, something I'm sure that old codger never would've believed possible.

I've never forgotten the valuable lesson I learned that day in 1974 from that old fisherman at the boat ramp. We must be very careful who we seek counsel from, otherwise we may become the brunt of someone else's joke, or even worse, we'll become the unsuspecting victim of someone's erroneous teaching. I was an ignorant novice in a foreign place using equipment I had not yet become accustomed to using. In my zeal I sought out counsel from what clearly looked like an expert, but instead my perceived 'expert' ended up being someone who made me out to be the 'fool'.

I have counseled hundreds of people who have been deeply wounded by the words of others who took them for a joy ride when the mosquitoes of circumstance were draining them dry of their life's blood. There's always a time and place for friends to have 'fun', but we must be careful to never have our 'fun' at the expense of someone else's weakness or ignorance. The 'old guys' of life never consider the sacrifices being made to learn how to excel at something you've never done. They never take into account where you've come from or what your purpose in being there might be. They will seize any opportunity to add another notch to their belt of practical jokes and gestures. In this life it's inevitable every one of us will at some point be taken for a 'ride'. When that happens we must be especially careful to not let the insensitivity of others steal our zeal to press on toward the goal and the prize we have set before us. We too easily lose heart over the swarming mosquitoes and self-promoting codgers sitting by the boat ramps of life.

While praying recently the Lord spoke to my heart and said, 'My son, you will never lead squadrons of eagles if you are continually distracted by the swarms of gnats.' That made me think of this story when I sat at the ramp being sucked dry by hundreds of mosquitoes while being taken for a 'ride'. That experience could have easily crushed my dreams and desires to be the best I could be as a fisherman, and to provide necessary food for my family. Instead, God supernaturally gave me the ability to use the experience as a stepping stone to greater success. The Holy Spirit continued to help me with His advice and counsel, but also led me to others who took great pleasure in teaching me more and more about 'fishing', not only for food, but for the souls of men. Eventually I became a personal guide teaching others how to 'fish' in the lakes and streams of Florida as well as life. I determined to never leave any disciple with nothing more than a well-seasoned board, but did everything I could to help fill their table with the delicacies of heaven.

In the days to come should you find yourself being taken for a 'ride' by an old guy at the dock, just slip away quietly and determine in your heart to never allow yourself to be offended. Otherwise, the old guy will continue to feed you 'boards' for years to come. If for some reason you have collected a lot of 'boards' over the years, then let me encourage you to immediately go out in your back yard and have a bonfire for Jesus. I would love to take you fishing and not only teach you how to catch 'big fish', but show you where all my 'honey holes' are. I will even provide the gear you need to fish with. Anyone want to go fishing today?

Prayer

O Father,

With a single word You create entire universes, so please help me today to speak only those words which build up, exalt and glorify You. So often I have eaten the bitter fruit of foolish, unnecessary and unwise conversations. Time and time again I seem to get caught up speaking about the swarming mosquitoes in my life rather than speaking by faith Your unchangeable words 'to' the momentary mountains of circumstance. Too often I find myself talking about You long before I have ever quietly spoken to You. I am truly a verbal spring that pours forth fresh and brackish water at the same time. O Father, set a guard over my tongue that I might speak only that which You have spoken beforehand. I am Your servant and messenger entrusted with a 'word' from heaven that has the power to set the captives of this present darkness free. From this day forth may my words be the glorious 'message' of heaven rather than the 'mess' of my idle thinking. Thank You for choosing me to be Your ambassador. Thank You for giving me the tongue of a disciple. Lead me to that place wherein the treasure of my heart and the fruit of my words are both in harmony with Your will and destiny for my life. Help me to be quick to hear, slow to speak and slow to anger. Deliver me from any future bitter harvest from unwise words I have spoken in haste in the past. Forgive me for using my tongue to promote my arguments and agendas rather than proclaiming Your heart and word to the nations. May my words continue to decrease and Your words increase in my spirit, heart and mind. Then I will speak a word in season that will bring about Your praise and glory. Once again I lay my heart and tongue on the altar of Your endless and matchless grace, mercy, forgiveness, patience and love. O Great Incarnate Word of heaven, fill me once again with Your thoughts that I may tell others the only Truth that will set them free. Amen.

And He said to them, "Follow Me, and I will make you fishers of men. Immediately, they left their nets and followed Him. Matthew 4:19-20 NASU

The Story Behind the Song:

If you've ever had a time in your life when everything seemed to be spiraling out of control, then you will understand where I was when I wrote *You Are My Keeper.* The lyrics to this song were birthed at a time when I desperately needed practical, godly answers to some very difficult situations that could no longer be put on the back burner or ignored. Although the ministry at that time had only a few staff members, I was reeling under the burden of feeling responsible for their well-being. Furthermore, two of my children had grown to the age where they were daily crossing all the boundaries we had placed within our home and I was struggling mightily with how to handle their continuous rebellion. What was I supposed to do? It seemed the more I looked for answers the more confused, weary and frustrated I became. Then one day the Lord's presence came in like a mighty rushing wind assuring me He was still with me and in full control. His simple words to me that day were, 'Son, I am your Keeper'. I would love to report to you that soon after writing this song my children became model citizens and the ministry was blessed with an abundance of finances which relieved all the pressure concerning the daily needs of the staff. None of that happened, but a heavenly peace settled in my heart that caused all the confusion to disappear (for a little while). If you are presently in a similar place of weariness and confusion, I pray the words to *You Are My Keeper* brings you the same peace I received that day when God assured me that He is and always will be my KEEPER.

Psalm 121 *I will lift up my eyes to the mountains; From where shall my help come? 2 My help comes from the Lord, Who made heaven and earth. 3 He will not allow your foot to slip; He who keeps you will not slumber. 4 Behold, He who keeps Israel will neither slumber nor sleep. 5 The Lord is your keeper; The Lord is your shade on your right hand. 6 The sun will not smite you by day, nor the moon by night. 7 The Lord will protect you from all evil; He will keep your soul. 8 The Lord will guard your going out and your coming in from this time forth and forever.* NASU

You Are My Keeper
(Song from the Give Them Back project, music and lyrics written by Jerry Williams)

When I don't know which way to turn, I know You'll protect me.
When I don't know which way is right, You lead me on.
In the heat of the day You're always there to cover me,
You are my Keeper! You are my Lord!

Throughout the seasons of my heart, You're always near me.
Through the times of bitter cold, You keep me warm.
When the eyes of my spirit can't seem to clearly see You,
You are my Keeper! You are my Lord!

Chorus:
So my God, unto You...I will sing!
My God, unto You I give the glory!
With my heart, with my mouth I will give You praise!
You are my Keeper! You are my Lord!

When I don't know the reasons why, I know You'll teach me.
And when I question what You've done, You never leave.
Through the times of despair, times I can't hear You calling,
You are my Keeper! You are my Lord!

Chorus:
So my God, unto You...I will sing!
My God, unto You I give the glory!
With my heart, with my mouth I will give You praise!
You are my Keeper! You are my Lord!

DAY 21 AN ENCOUNTER WITH HELL

Behold, I have given you authority to tread upon serpents and scorpions, and overcome all the power of the enemy, and nothing shall by any means injure you. Luke 10:19

It was the spring of 1972 and I was in my second year as a student at Oral Roberts University. I had transferred to ORU a year earlier after completing two years of Jr. College in Odessa, Texas. Being a transfer student I was older than most of the other guys in my dorm. As a result, it didn't take long before I became a 'big brother' to many of those who were struggling with being home sick. Although I was still a new believer (born again in September of 1970), I was consumed with an insatiable hunger for the presence and knowledge of our awesome God. Surprisingly, ORU at that time was much like any other college campus having only a remnant of students who were genuinely passionate about their destiny and pursuit of the Lord. Consequently, living on campus provided tremendous opportunities for personal ministry which was greatly supported by the leadership of the University who continuously encouraged us to be bold in our faith and unapologetically open in our love and witness for Christ.

During the spring semester of 1972, while I was praying and fasting seeking a greater anointing in my life, I unexpectedly encountered a demonic presence in one of the younger students on the second floor of the dormitory where I was living. I had just left my room and was walking down the hallway to meet someone already waiting for me in the lobby, when suddenly the door to one of the rooms I was passing by violently burst open. One of the young men who occupied that room (John) somehow mysteriously knew I was approaching his door at that exact moment.

As soon as his eyes connected with mine he jumped in front of me intentionally blocking the hallway refusing to let me pass. John was from New York and like me, was a transfer student, but this was his first semester at ORU and his first time to be away from home. Normally he was a quiet and extremely introverted guy who was rarely seen or heard from on the floor. I had met and briefly spoken to him on a few occasions and had been specifically praying for him that day. The majority of the other students avoided any personal contact with him because he suffered with one of the worst cases of facial acne I had ever seen. I'm not talking about a few bumps and ugly pimples, but the kind of physical condition that needs to be continually wiped due to the fluids running out of the sores on his face. As he boldly stood blocking any attempt to pass by it soon became clear he was being controlled by a demonic power that was seeking a confrontation with me. Since I was already late for my meeting downstairs I attempted to graciously slip around him to honor my previous commitment. Becoming even more determined to not let me pass, John raised his voice in opposition, but the voice I heard coming forth from him was not of this world. I immediately stopped and with a holy boldness looked straight into the eyes of this tormented young man.

What transpired over the next two hours was one of the first dramatic encounters I have experienced with the forces of hell and darkness. Not wanting to draw attention to the situation (the devil loves attention and will do almost anything to draw a crowd), I quickly stepped into his room and closed the door. Instantly the demon within him proclaimed, 'You can't have him! He's mine!' (It's important to remember I had been praying and fasting all week asking the Lord for a greater anointing and manifestation of His power and authority in and through my life.) For nearly two hours I wrestled with the principalities and powers of this present world darkness who had taken dominion over John's life. I never once felt frightened or believed I was in danger, but with a God inspired certainty I rested in the truth that 'greater is He that is in me than he that is in the world'. The demonic forces possessing John continuously threatened to kill both of us (this is common when dealing with the demonic), but a peace and calmness kept me focused and ready with a Word from heaven. I wish I could tell you John was delivered from his bondage and torment that night, but that simply didn't happen. However, there was a tremendous breakthrough as well as a strong foundation of TRUTH established in his life during those nearly two hours that made preparation for his soon coming deliverance, freedom and salvation.

Two or three days later (I was still fasting and praying) I received an unexpected phone call around 10:00 p.m. from St. Luke's Hospital. The nurse calling shared that she had just acquired my phone number from a young ORU student who had earlier that evening overdosed and was not expected to survive the night. That student was none other than John. Since his family was in New York and obviously could not get there in time, he had given them my name and number to call. I quickly got myself together, then asked two other young men who radically loved Jesus to go with me to the hospital. It took about thirty minutes before we made our way across town to the hospital.

As soon as we arrived the same nurse I had earlier spoken to reluctantly explained they had done everything medically possible to save John's life, but it was basically too late as the drugs he ingested had already spread throughout his system. In short, we were told there was nothing else that could medically be done for him and it was only a matter of time before they expected him to simply shut down and quit breathing. A righteous anger rose up in my spirit as I knew the devil was trying to make good on his earlier threat to kill John. I also knew none of what was happening was a coincidence, and understood God had placed John directly in my path to see His glory and praise manifested through this entire potentially deadly situation. As we entered the private room John lying flat on the bed in a semi-conscious state. The rails on the bed had been raised to the maximum height to insure he wouldn't fall onto the floor as a result of the violent convulsions he was experiencing from the drugs that were now ravaging his body. As the two brothers with me were making their way to the opposite side of the bed, I walked directly over to John's bed and reached over the extended rail placing my right hand on his chest. I did this simply to let him know I was there beside him.

My only thought in that moment was to attempt to calm him down and give him some assurance he was no longer alone. Placing my hand on his convulsing chest I said the words, 'In the name of Jesus!' Instantaneously John's body sprang straight up bringing us face to face. Seconds before he was in a semi-conscious convulsive state, but now we were staring into each other's eyes in surprise and amazement. (I was literally hanging over the rail on my tip toes preparing to pray for him.) Then without any warning he opened his mouth and every ounce of the deadly poison ravaging his body gushed forth from the depths of his innermost being forcibly spewing out of his mouth. One moment he was violently convulsing as his body struggled to stay alive, then in an instant he was gloriously delivered and totally healed. The only unfortunate thing that transpired in the midst of this miraculous demonstration of the power of the name of Jesus was what physically happened to me. Dangling directly in front of him I caught the full brunt of his deliverance. I tried to throw myself out of the path of the deadly emulsions that came spewing out of his mouth, but to no avail. Being drenched with the putrid poison I never personally witnessed most of what took place next. The two brothers with me excitedly related how John leaped out of the bed ripping away all the tubes connected to his body. He then joyously ran out into the hallway shouting praises to the Lord wearing nothing but his hospital gown. His hands were raised in praise to our mighty God as he continued shouting the name of Jesus! Meanwhile, I was dry heaving and gagging back in the room trying to determine how to successfully remove the T-shirt I was wearing that was now soaked with the manifestations of John's deliverance. I finally just bit the bullet and pulled it off over my face and head. All I can say is it was a good thing I had been fasting all week and had nothing in my stomach. Praise the Lord for even small blessings.

Several days later I realized the Lord had powerfully answered my prayers for a greater anointing in my life, but He did so in a way I was not considering or expecting. His power and authority were manifested in and through my life in ways I had never previously seen or experienced. Furthermore, I learned several invaluable lessons that have stayed with me throughout my years in the ministry. I learned I must stay on the alert and never, never, never focus on the words being spoken to me by the enemy, or anyone else being manipulated by the enemy. Secondly I learned that every thought must be taken captive and brought into obedience to the Lordship of Jesus. These lessons will never be maintained unless I diligently feed and focus on His Word. Thirdly, I learned there is no substitute for hiding the Word of God in your heart. The enemy will not be patient while you try and remember where a certain scripture might be located. Memorization of the scriptures is not important, IT IS ESSENTIAL for all those who desire to be followers and disciples of the Lord Jesus. Lastly, I realized my opinions may be words that have some measure of wisdom or knowledge, but they have no power or authority over the enemy. However, the Word of God, which is the undefeatable sword of the Spirit, is an indestructible weapon that will never be successfully challenged or conquered. The more proficient I become in my use of this heavenly weapon the more effective I will be as a warrior of God. Ultimately it's never about me, but all about Christ in me, the Hope of glory and salvation. He is the living, incarnate Word of God. I am an unworthy, yet highly favored son of God who has been mercifully delivered out of darkness and graciously chosen to be an ambassador of His Light to all the world. Thank You, Jesus!

I saw John many times during the rest of that year and he always had a smile on his face and a bounce in his step. I didn't return to school after that next summer as the Lord led me into the ministry, but I am confident John went forth to lead a life full of blessing and favor in the presence of our awesome Deliverer and Savior! To God be all the glory and praise!

Whenever I share this glorious story of John's deliverance and salvation, I am shocked to find that today the overwhelming majority of my brothers and sisters in Christ have had little personal experience in dealing with the forces of hell and darkness. How can this be when the very essence of who we are in Christ is in direct opposition to everything that is in the world? I simply can't fathom how we who are 'LIGHT' do not find ourselves in continual confrontation with the forces of 'DARKNESS'. The purpose of 'LIGHT' is to expose what is in the 'DARK'. For years I have prayed God would cause me to be known in hell as a 'man of God'. Let me say again, I do not understand how we who are called to be the 'light of the world' do not have continual encounters with the forces of darkness. I cannot sit idly by while darkness slowly encroaches and overcomes my neighborhood, my children, my city, my state or our nation. It's time to beat our plowshares into swords and rise up as one man seeing the victory of the Lord manifest again in our homes, cities, states and nations. The motto of the U.S. Army is 'Be All that You Can Be!' It's time for us as children of God to believe and 'Be All that We Can Be' in the name of Jesus!

Prayer

O Great Warrior of heaven and Keeper of my soul, I bow before You as my Commander and Chief, and the Captain of my soul. Fill me with Your strength and courage that I might be a faithful warrior ready to do Your bidding and will. Should darkness try to slip past my guard, give me keen eyes to detect its presence and a ready heart to drive out the intruder without mercy or any consideration of what it may offer to my carnal flesh. Flood my heart and soul with Your presence and power that I might ever be an impassioned warrior living and serving You only. Purify my love for You that I might continually be Your son and soldier who lives with a holy hatred of evil. May others who see me find encouragement to confidently stand against the forces of this present world darkness. As a soldier of Light, may I be honored in Your presence with the task of leading multitudes out of darkness into Your marvelous Light. Help me to serve You not only out of duty, but also out of love that issues forth from a heart that once was bound, but now is free. Thank You for reaching into the dark abyss of my own rebellion and rescuing me from being forever enslaved to wickedness. Were it not for You and the blood of Your Son, my Savior and Captain, I would have never known the joy of being Your adopted son, and a soldier of Your righteousness. My life is now wholly committed to You, Your service, Your will and Your pleasure. Do all that is in Your heart with the rest of my life and may the kingdom of hell suffer great loss because of Your Life within me, Your servant. Here am I, Lord! Send me! Amen.

The Story Behind the Song:

I wrote *Hold On* at a time in my life when the Lord was giving me several songs to rally the soldiers of God to unite, stand and FIGHT the good FIGHT of faith. On the same recording project (Mighty River) was another song entitled *I Won't Be Denied* that was similar in its message and purpose. By the time I had completed writing the songs for the *Mighty River* project I was physically, mentally and spiritually exhausted from being on what felt like the front lines of a multi-year war with the kingdom of darkness. By the grace of God through all the struggles, spiritual casualties, betrayals and personal setbacks we still were eyewitnesses to tens of thousands coming to Christ. Hallelujah! No matter how hard it seemed to get, the presence of God, the lives being radically transformed, and the certainty of the call and destiny of God in our lives kept us firmly implanted in the mission and ministry God had anointed us to accomplish for His glory. At the same time I was seeing an alarming trend taking place that had gone almost unnoticed by the majority of others I knew in the ministry. That trend was the number of people leaving the ministry each year due to what was being called 'burn out'. As I struggled to understand how anyone could 'burn out' if they remained in the FIRE OF HIS PRESENCE, the Lord graciously gave me *Hold On* as an anthem and challenge specifically to those leaders who were considering quitting. My cry to them was HOLD ON! Quit your grumbling and complaining and look up! Jesus has that old devil on the run. DON'T GIVE UP! If you are one of those who have become disillusioned in the ministry and are considering quitting, then even today I have this word for you: HOLD ON! JESUS WILL GET HIM AND IT WON'T BE LONG! HOLD ON! Lift your eyes up and see the One Who has called you to this marvelous destiny. He has never left you and NEVER WILL! It's time for that old serpent to get a fresh dose of Holy Ghost pain!

<u>Hold On</u>
(Song from the Mighty River project written by Jerry Williams)

Chorus:
Hold on! Hold on! Jesus, He will get him and it won't be long!
Hold on! Hold on! Jesus, He will get him and it won't be long!

If the devil's got you thinking it's going to be bad
He knows that you've been listening to lies in your head

He promises he'll give you anything you want
Then sends a fallen angel to destroy your home

He takes his wicked finger, sticks it in your heart
Heats it up inside and makes a fiery dart
Tells you every day you're going to die in sin
Wants you to believe you can never win, never win.

Hold on! Hold on! Jesus, He will get him and it won't be long!
Hold on! Hold on! Jesus, He will get him and it won't be long!

Well, it's easier to grumble than it is to be good
When you're living in a jungle full of negative food
Nobody ever said that it'd be easy to win
But what a stupid reason to give up or given in!

If I were you I'd start to make a positive change
'Cause the devil's going to get a dose of Holy Ghost pain
Rivers of love are going to fall from the sky
Then people who are dead in every city and town...Hallelujah!
They're going to rise!

Chorus:

DAY 22 KNOWN BY OUR COLOR

I want to begin by making a statement that might surprise you, but is none the less true: COLOR MATTERS in this world, and also in the world to come. Now let me explain what I mean. First let's consider three separate areas wherein 'color' matters and affects this present world we live in.

1. The first area supporting my premise (COLOR MATTERS) finds its life in the ugly arena of personal PREJUDICE. Far too often we have all seen PREJUDICE violently displayed in the news media outlets around our ever shrinking world. The truth is, until this world and all that is in it is eventually destroyed by the breath of God's fiery judgment, prejudice will remain an ugly stronghold among those who live in it. I know all too well how prejudice over the 'color' of one's skin can affect every part of your daily life. I grew up in the West Texas town of Odessa in a time when students, families and friends were legally separated by the COLOR of their skin. We lived on the outskirts of the far West side of town where the majority of the middle class and lower income families lived. Consequently, this meant there were a lot of kids close to my neighborhood who weren't 'white'. For us (the kids) it made absolutely no difference what 'color' another kid's skin was. All we cared about was if they could play ball or not. You see, in those days (1950's and 1960's) athletics was a big part of just about every kid's daily life. Video

games, computers, arcades, cell phones and sprawling neighborhood malls didn't exist yet. Therefore, kids spent the bulk of their time outside playing any kind of sport that required the use of a 'ball'. In those days 'being outside' didn't mean staying in the safety and confines of your yard. The entire neighborhood was our playground. And, because we all had bicycles, it was nothing for us to ride fifteen or twenty blocks to the nearest park or school ground to play 'ball'. I have such great memories of riding my bike day after day to the West County Park where there would always be a lot of other guys there playing ball, and a lot of those guys were not white. Thankfully we never got swept up in all the hoopla about the COLOR of the other guys' skin, but just had fun playing together. Unfortunately, that wasn't how it was once we left the park. During that time all throughout the south signs blanketed town after town with prejudiced statements such as, 'Whites Only', 'No Blacks Allowed'. Even our schools back then were specifically built to maintain separation between the Hispanics, Black Americans and whites. Gratefully that brutal era of legalized segregation has long since been abolished.

Even though the Civil Rights Movement abolished legalized segregation in America, prejudice still thrives in the hearts of multitudes who are living in darkness and ignorance. Honestly, as a young kid I never really understood what the words *prejudice* or *segregation* really meant. All I knew was those were the words being used that oftentimes kept me from playing 'ball' with several of my best friends such as Pookie and Johnny, and I didn't like it one bit.

It took several more years before I was finally able to see and understand the bitter root of ignorance permeating the minds of so many of my generation which led to the horrifying manifestations of prejudice I've already mentioned. Sadly, I didn't have to look very far to find that some of the most prejudiced people in my city were members of my own family who actually believed 'whites' were created by God as a superior race over those of darker 'color'. By the grace of God that kind of warped thinking never took root in my mind or heart.

What a great and pivotal day in our nation when segregation was eventually legally abolished and the words of the late Martin Luther King, *I have a dream*, became the platform for a new beginning for all present and future citizens of our nation, no matter the COLOR of their skin. Today at The FORT Discipleship Center we are reaping the benefits and blessings of that glorious decision. At The FORT (our home church in Houston, Texas) we have been honored and blessed to have multiple nations represented in our membership. Should you come to worship with us you will see white, black and brown brothers and sisters in Christ singing and shouting together the praises of our mighty God without prejudice of any kind. This kind of corporate gathering would have been an impossibility when I was a young boy. Thankfully the 'color' barrier has been broken (but not yet fully eradicated) and we are growing as a nation and as a 'church' in our understanding of how to live and work together in harmony.

2. Now that you've been exposed to some of my personal roots, let's further consider the subject of 'color' from another perspective. This revelation came to me while I was in Amarillo, Texas one morning spending time praying and studying the book of Isaiah. Suddenly the presence of God manifested like a thick cloud inside the little barrio house we were temporarily using as an office while ministering in the Panhandle of Texas. The following scriptures exploded off the page that morning as I read them:

> *Speak comfort to Jerusalem, and cry out to her, that her warfare is ended, that her iniquity is pardoned; For she has received from the LORD's hand double for all her sins.* Isaiah 40:2
>
> *You whom I have taken from the ends of the earth, and called from its farthest regions, and said to you, 'You are My servant, I have chosen you and have not cast you away: Fear not, for I am with you; Be not dismayed, for I am your God. I will strengthen you, yes, I will help you, I will uphold you with My righteous right hand.' Behold, all those who were incensed against you shall be ashamed and disgraced; They shall be as nothing, and those who strive with you shall perish. You shall seek them and not find them--Those who contended with you. Those who war against you shall be as nothing, as a nonexistent thing. For I, the LORD your God, will hold your right hand, saying to you, 'Fear not, I will help you.'* Isaiah 41:9-13

My joyous shouts were literally resounding throughout the small 800 square foot building as the Lord met with me that morning. Then I read this next verse which suddenly turned my praise into unsettled questioning:

Fear not, you worm Jacob, you men of Israel! I will help you, says the LORD and your Redeemer, the Holy One of Israel. Isaiah 41:14

I was completely confused as to why the Lord suddenly diverted from lavishing promises of imminent restoration and future hope on Jacob to now identify him with his past failures by unmercifully calling him a "worm". All I could do in that moment was sit and stare at the words: *..you worm, Jacob.* The longer I wrestled with these words, I began to realize there had to be a lack of understanding on my part because what I was thinking in that moment was in direct contradiction to the unfathomable riches of the mercy of God I had experienced time and again. I am a blessed recipient of the mercy and forgiveness of God's unconditional LOVE and know with certainty He would never proclaim our confessed sins to be forever cleansed, forgiven and forgotten, and then bring them back up again sometime in the future to harm or condemn us in any way. GOD CANNOT LIE, and He distinctly promises if we confess our sins HE CASTS OUR CONFESSED SINS AS FAR AS THE EAST IS FROM THE WEST! (Psalms 103:8-12) Hallelujah! THERE IS NO CONDEMNATION IN CHRIST! He is faithful to forgive us all our sins (1 John 1:9)! Consequently, I quietly leaned back in my chair and cried out to the Holy Spirit for greater revelation. As I pondered the reality that none of us could ever hope to fulfill His destiny in our lives if we didn't have confidence we were truly forgiven and freed from the bondage and condemnation of our former rebellion, suddenly the revelation came. Praise the Lord! Within moments the Holy Spirit opened my understanding and poured into my spirit an amazingly wonderful revelation, and it is completely centered upon 'color'.

What I learned that glorious morning was this: When God referred to Jacob as a "worm" He wasn't pointing to his past, but was rather pointing to his eternal lineage and heritage in Christ. When God referred to Jacob as a 'worm', He was specifically identifying him (Jacob) with the "scarlet worm". As I looked deeper into the significance of why God identified Jacob with the 'scarlet worm' I learned some amazing things. When the scarlet worm is ready to give birth to her young, she unselfishly sacrifices her own life by permanently attaching herself to the trunk of a tree. In so doing she creates a protective shield for the otherwise vulnerable and helpless young. As she sacrifices her own life through attaching herself to die on a tree, she then excretes a crimson dye-like substance that saturates the large area of the trunk where she willingly died for her young. The result of her unselfish sacrifice was a large, brilliant scarlet colored residue easily visible on the trunk of the tree. In the days when this 'word' was written to Jacob it was common practice to extract the bright red substance from the bark of the tree then use it to create the rich color of the commercially retailed scarlet materials that were so valuable in the trade markets of the world at that time.

In Psalms 22:6 the Spirit prophetically speaks through David about One Who would willingly give Himself up for His offspring by permanently attaching Himself to a tree called Calvary. Through the shedding of His precious blood He would thereby completely cover our sins and provide through His death the heavenly nutrients necessary to strengthen us through our walk here until we see Him again in glory. Hallelujah! Jacob, 'stained' forever in the Spirit by the brilliant scarlet color of His Redeemer, was being identified as the offspring of heaven. This heavenly affirmation and identification forever shut the mouth of his accusers who would so quickly remind him of his past. That is precisely why God changed his name from Jacob to Israel.

With that wonderful thought in mind consider that from the moment you enter the earth until the day you are wrapped in the chrysalis of death you will be identified in the flesh first and foremost by your color. Throughout society the simple truth is...color matters. I sometimes wonder if God doesn't often look upon the sons of men with great pleasure seeing us as a beautiful multi-colored bouquet with each individual plant having its own special color and beauty for all to behold. Thankfully we are past the ignorant days of bigotry and segregation based on the 'color' of one's skin. However, the 'color' of your heart is a matter that will determine your eternal place of habitation. Can others see the brilliant 'scarlet color' of the Love of God flowing from your life and heart? That LOVE freely attached Himself to a tree for 'you'. If you willingly come under the loving control, protection and benefits of His sacrifice, then you will forever be known and recognized by the crimson 'stain' of His shed blood that covers all your former 'stains'.

3. Finally, there is a third area I want to mention concerning 'color'. In the ever-growing world of motorcyclists and bikers, the "patch" that is worn on their backs is normally referred to as their "colors". In the dangerous and wicked world of outlaw bikers it is not uncommon to hear of rival club members fighting to the death for the right to wear and defend their "colors". Rejoice O struggling and embattled believer. There is One Who has already victoriously fought for your right to "wear His colors" and thereby be forever marked and known as a lifetime member of His family. Therefore, when the voices around you begin to maliciously point the finger at your former failures attempting to disqualify you because of your past, rise up and confidently display your 'colors'. That crimson stain that now covers you from head to toe will proclaim in their hearing, 'This worm is destined to be resurrected in inexpressible beauty (like a butterfly) to soar forever in the vastness of God's eternal love! In Him I'm accepted!'

Prayer

O Father,

I understand and acknowledge that You created every color for Your purpose and pleasure. Give me Your eyes to behold the wonders and beauty of every tribe, tongue, people and nation. Take from my heart and mind any remaining residue of prejudice and favoritism I may have formerly embraced because of the color of someone's skin. May I be a worthy bearer of the scarlet color that flowed from the veins of Your only begotten Son and now drips from the mercy seat of heaven. Forgive me, Lord, for too often ignorantly flaunting the colors of heaven in places that do not glorify or exalt You. I am ashamed to acknowledge times I have ventured into new endeavors and projects without openly bearing the crimson colors of my Savior, Jesus Christ. From this day forth I lay down the colors of my own agendas, and with a holy resolve I choose to unceasingly bear the colors of my eternal lineage and heritage. May all those I encounter in the days to come see from a distance the crimson markings of the blood of Jesus permeating and saturating my life. Should there be any clothes in the closets of my heart that do not bear these colors, then give me the courage to throw them into the sea of forgotten memories. O Lamb of God, thank You for covering me with the blood stained robe of Your righteousness. As one would send an aromatic and beautiful bouquet of flowers to those who are hurting and downcast, send me forth into the world for Your glory and praise alone. Thank You for extracting me from the dungeons of everlasting darkness wherein the colors of death and eternal damnation are forever embedded in the souls of the sons of disobedience. Thank You for changing my lineage and heritage. Thank You for choosing me to bear the colors that reflect the beauty of Your holiness. Although I know I am unworthy of such an honor, I gladly accept that I am Your appointed courier wearing and bearing Your colors. For all who would set their gaze upon these colors I now joyfully bear, there lies an open invitation to cast down their present worldly colors and join with me in bearing the scarlet colors of Your Son's blood, shed for the sins of every man. I love and praise You, O Lord! Amen.

The Story Behind the Song:

The song *When I Look In Your Word* may seem like a strange fit for this devotional, but it's actually perfect. The living Word of God is actively working in our hearts, minds and spirits dividing out the fleshly thoughts and intentions from the Spirit's thoughts and intentions. The more the Word gets implanted in us, the more we will see things the way God sees them. To see with the eyes of God eliminates all prejudice and embraces every human being as a fearfully and wonderfully crafted creation of God, no matter what their COLOR. God loves all people of all COLORS equally, and so should we as His children. If this is an area you still struggle with, then the first thing you need to do is start saturating your mind with the Word of God. His words are Life and Truth and will bring an eternal perspective to your life that may not exist right now. The Word has become my daily food and drink, and I cannot maintain a right mind without its heavenly nutrients giving health to the thoughts and intentions of my heart. Thank You, Jesus, for Your precious promises through which I can become a partaker of the nature of God.

I will give thanks to You, for I am fearfully and wonderfully made;
Wonderful are Your works, And my soul knows it very well.
My frame was not hidden from You, When I was made in secret,
And skillfully wrought in the depths of the earth;
Your eyes have seen my unformed substance;
And in Your book were all written
The days that were ordained for me,
When as yet there was not one of them.
Psalm 139:14-16 NASU

When I Look in Your Word
(Song from the Carry On project, music and lyrics written by Jerry Williams)

When I look in Your Word, O the things You help me to see
And the things I've heard
Make me feel like crying, make me feel like flying
Away with You

When I look in Your Word suddenly the things
That have always conquered me
Fall into the sea of forgotten memories
'Cause they're covered by Your love

Chorus:
O Lord, give me now the heart to forever follow You
O Lord, give me the desire

Eyes so full of fire
I will only, only, only follow You

When I look in Your Word time and time again
I can hear You speak to me
Telling me be strong! Telling me go on!
Telling me You won't ever leave! No! No!

When I look in Your Word I feel the dirty waters
Of trouble leaving me
Giving the control of my body and my soul
To the God Who set me free

Chorus
O Lord, give me now the heart to forever follow You
O Lord, give me the desire
Eyes so full of fire
I will only, only, only follow You

DAY 23 TRY, TRY, TRY AGAIN

For a righteous man falls seven times, and rises again, but the wicked stumble in time of calamity. Proverbs 24:16

I'm not sure exactly what age I was at the time (probably six or seven), but I can easily remember the moment I came running out and gazed upon my first bicycle. For the last several months I had been hoping this would be the year I would get a new bicycle for Christmas. Even though I was very young, I knew for this to happen would take a sort of miracle since my parents were doing all they could to just keep us fed and clothed. Well, the miracle had happened and there it was standing upright in all its glory and beauty only a few feet in front of me. It was a brilliant coal black colored frame with chrome accessories and spoked wheels. It was hands down the most amazing and awesome thing I had ever owned. I'm certain most of you can remember times as a kid when you experienced overwhelming excitement and inexpressible joy in moments like these. That's what happened to me that glorious morning, but the exhilaration and joy would soon be accompanied by a paralyzing fear of the unknown. You see, I was the only guy left in the neighborhood 'gang' who didn't yet have a bike of his own. Now all that had changed! No longer would the 'gang' fly by me as I walked to and from school every day.

My biggest dream had now come true and this was the 'day' I would finally be riding with the 'gang'. There was just one small obstacle I needed to get past - I didn't have a clue how to ride a bicycle. No problem, right? I mean, how hard could it be? As soon as we had all finished opening our gifts (it was Christmas morning), I quickly guided my chariot out into the middle of 19th street. I stood for a few moments basking in the glory and hoping everyone in the neighborhood would see me with my new 'ride'. For the first few moments there was absolutely no thought of failure in my mind, but only an unwavering determination to do whatever it would take to soon be riding like the wind through my neighborhood.

It's important to let you know that back in those days it was common for the guys in the 'gang' to each pretend to be some kind of super hero. It was amazing how often we strutted around acting like 'super men' in little boy bodies. That, of course, meant if I was going to really be 'super', then I could NEVER, EVER learn how to ride my new bike with those sissy training wheels attached on the back. (All the bikes came with training wheels in the box.) Even though I had never been on a bicycle, I was determined no one was ever going to see me with those 'sissy wheels' on my bike. After all, everyone knew that training wheels were for girls, sissies and wimps, right? Consequently, my first several attempts to mount my new chariot made it painfully obvious why training wheels were included and why they would have made things much, much easier.

Another important fact to know is my parents had purposefully bought a bicycle I could 'grow into' and would hopefully be able to ride for several years. I'm sure they thought that was a good plan, but the main problem facing me at that particular moment was trying to figure out how to mount the giant chariot, much less ride it with the 'gang'. I first tried placing it in the street next to the curb, but found it was still too tall for me. I tried pushing it down the street with the idea I would mount it while it was already moving. That was a really bad idea. I finally figured out the only thing I could do was lean it up against the chain link fence, then climb on using the fence as a ladder. Once I determined how to mount my new 'ride', I boldly made my first attempt to pedal down the sidewalk with the fence on one side and the dangerous curb on the other side. I don't remember how many times I crashed, but it was so many it left me scraped and bruised for weeks. Had I been able to mount the bicycle while it was already on the street I'm sure the crashes wouldn't have been so brutal. Each time I fell I would peel myself off the pavement bearing some newly formed battle scar from yet another failed launch attempt. Whether the cavernous street on my left or the chain link fence on my right, each fall took its bloody, painful toll. I can still see in my mind's eye some of the terrible looking scabs that formed over the many scrapes and cuts that occurred with my multiple days of crashing. Each day, though, I would get a little further down the sidewalk until finally early one Saturday morning (long before anyone else had gotten out of bed) I glided down the sidewalk and eased out onto the street. Glory! I was riding, really riding, for the first time! That inexpressible joy I had known when I first saw my new 'steed' instantaneously flooded my soul again as I watched the curb go flying by. I had never had such a feeling of freedom. I was just about to shout in victory, but then I looked up. Because I had never safely made it off the sidewalk until that glorious morning, I had never actually 'maneuvered' the bicycle.

Now came the next test: Could I maneuver the bike without crashing? Panic and confusion took over my elation as I was picking up more and more speed. Four houses down Grady Boyd's dad's pickup was parked on the side of the street directly in my path. Do you know what it feels like to be on a moving object and be frozen with fear at the same time? That's exactly what happened to me. I froze in place as the bike continued to gain speed all the while racing toward the helpless, unsuspecting pickup. Then the inevitable happened. I slammed into the back bumper of the pickup and was instantly catapulted off the bike and over the side of the pickup. Amazingly I wasn't injured at all.

(I guess I had learned how to absorb a fall by that time.) As I picked myself up from the ground and turned around I saw an unbelievable sight: my bike had been going so fast the front wheel was now lodged under the bumper of the pickup thus becoming embarrassingly stuck. Even though I pulled with all my strength, I simply could not get the bike to dislodge from under the pickup's bumper. Then horror of horrors, Grady's dad saw what happened and came walking out the front door. I went pale white in about one second as he approached. Thankfully he wasn't angry, but was concerned that I was alright. Once he was certain I wasn't hurt, he carefully pulled the hopelessly damaged front wheel out from under his undamaged bumper. I profusely apologized, then dejectedly pushed the broken chariot back uphill toward my home. However, my dejection was short-lived as I realized just how far I had actually gone before crashing. In that moment, just after suffering the worst wreck in my life, something unexplainable happened in my heart. Somehow in the wake of my greatest (and most embarrassing) bike-riding failure I was filled with the belief and confidence I could ride and not only survive, but be as good, or even better at riding than all my neighborhood buddies. By the time I got home I was re-energized with excitement and ran inside to tell everyone how far I had gone. Even though I had crashed and suffered a significant setback, I knew victory was now well within my grasp. I couldn't wait to get a new wheel and get back on the bike. Within less than a week the new wheel was securely in place and soon after I was flying through the neighborhood. It wasn't long after that I could be seen doing all sorts of tricks on my oversize chariot with that shiny new front wheel.

I often tell people who are going through really difficult circumstances that God never promised this life would be 'fair'. However, He did promise to give us the ability 'in Christ' to be victorious and more than conquerors. It is inevitable that 'falls' are going to come. Sometimes those falls result in some really ugly scabs being formed. One might even end up with several scars through the process. It's your choice whether these scars become reminders of your failures or testimonies of a 'never give up, never quit' spirit. Which one of these statements describes you today? Are you one of those who have dejectedly pushed your damaged bike back up the hill and decided to never get on it again? If so, let me encourage you to go get it out of the shed and I'll help you get it fixed. You were created to 'ride like the wind' through the neighborhoods of your life. Sure there are pitfalls and dangers all around, but you are created to soar past those without fear. Are you one of those who became so wounded you actually got rid of your bike? If so, come on over to my house. I will let you ride my bike and I will even run alongside while you re-learn how to ride a God size chariot again. I won't let you fall and crash, but will keep you going until you get the hang of it. What do you say? Let's go for a 'ride'!

Prayer

Mighty God, Strength and Sustainer of my soul, thank You for lifting me out of the miry clay of mediocrity and man size agendas. Thank You for equipping me with everything I need to accomplish Your will and purpose for my life. Thank You for creating within me abilities and talents that will be worthy allies to Your purpose and plan for my life. Thank You for standing beside me as my Teacher patiently instructing me through every fall and mishap I encounter or create through my own ignorance. Guard my mind and heart from ever thinking the way is too hard, too long, too dangerous or too costly. No matter how many difficulties may come, help me to persevere and finish the course You have set before me. By Your grace use my life to lead a multitude of others who have fallen along the way back to the highway of holiness. Implant within me the heart of a champion who worships before Your throne before ever engaging the enemy or trying to accomplish any 'thing' for You. Thank You for healing my wounded heart, then speaking Your words of kindness, hope and future victory over my soul. With You as my Guide and Teacher, victory is imminent and all things are possible. Amen.

The Story Behind the Song:

In 1990, I was a dad dealing with a sixteen-year-old who was seemingly falling off her bike (making mistake after mistake) every day. Most days I felt completely helpless not knowing how to guide or even protect her. Every day I would cry out to the Lord on her behalf, but as her daddy, I wanted to rush in and drive out the wicked giants invading her precious mind and heart. The problem was simple, she wouldn't let me in. Feeling totally useless, I finally locked myself in my writing room in an attempt to find some relief from the smothering cloud of confusion that was hanging over both of our lives. Like an Indian summer's day in winter the Lord began to speak directly to my heart concerning her, her future and her HOPE. *You've Got to Believe* is the song the Lord had me write from His heart to my precious daughter. For that reason, this song will always be one of those rare and special gifts of God to my life, and will hold a much higher place than hundreds of other songs I have written through the years. My hope and prayer is she will one day listen again to the words the Lord said to her so long ago as she has fallen off her bike again. I love you, sis.

You've Got to Believe

(Song from 41 Will Come project, music and lyrics written by Jerry Williams)

When your world comes crashing in, you can't put it back again
The rivers of your strong desire
flood your mind and drag you down
All the voices deep inside say, 'What's the use in trying?'
Everything you thought you learned lies motionless and dying

When the wind of change is strong, you can't make it on your own
You try to sleep, but lie awake, praying through your pillow case

Wondering if He still can hear you crying
Hoping in your heart there's still a chance He can

Chorus:
You've got to believe He will be there to heal your wounded heart
O believe, He'll never leave you all alone
You've got to believe He will forgive no matter what you've done
O believe...

When you've given in to fear, you can't find a friend who cares
Still you try to ease the pain by making artificial plans
All the voices in your mind say, 'What's the use in trying?'
You struggle with the truth you know that's fighting for your life

Chorus
All the voices in your mind say, 'What's the use in trying?'
You struggle with the truth you know that's fighting for your life

DAY 24 A MISTAKEN IDENTITY

For as he thinks in his heart, so is he. Proverbs 23:7

It was late spring in the mid 1990's and we were on tour in the Midwest region of the country. For those of you who have ever traveled through the Midwest during the late Spring and early summer, you know all too well that for hundreds of miles you see nothing but a seemingly endless stream of corn and bean fields with an occasional lake or river thrown in for good measure. We had driven all day before finally arriving in Ft. Wayne, Indiana where we were to be in concert that evening. Soon after the concert began the presence of God manifested in such a powerful way hundreds of people began flooding the front of the auditorium spontaneously making the area in front of the stage an altar to the Lord. What a glorious sight! What an awesome night that no one wanted to end! Several hours later as we were loading up the equipment we were all sharing testimonies about the more than two hundred people who had made some kind of significant decision for the Lord that night. The following story is a testimony of one of those life changing decisions made that night.

It was just after 9:00 p.m. when the concert officially ended, but the anointing and ministry of the Holy Spirit was long from being over. The counselors were still fully engaged in praying for the throng that had come forward, and everywhere you looked people were still crying out to the Lord for mercy, grace and forgiveness. It was one of those rare occasions when no one was concerned about the time or interested in leaving the auditorium. Hallelujah! I remained on the stage talking and praying with dozens who were lingering up front in this glorious presence. Suddenly, I was interrupted by two of the volunteer counselors who were visibly distraught about something. One of them boldly approached me and said, "We have a situation in the counseling room that needs your immediate attention". Without hesitation I followed the two anxious counselors who quickly led me to the farthest section of the counseling area. We then entered a large makeshift room that had been set up with temporary portable partitions which offered a measure of privacy for those needing to pray through some difficult things in their lives. Once we were all in the room I stopped for a moment to try and gain some discernment as to what could only be described as a very strange sight.

By this time at least a dozen counselors had gathered in the large makeshift room, but they were all standing around the edge of the room while a very ominous looking man sat completely alone in the center of the room. The man sitting alone had come forward for prayer, but none of the counselors were willing to even approach him for fear of what he might do to them. Needless to say, by the time I arrived a spirit of fear had gripped the thoughts of the counselors and the enemy had the upper hand. Without hesitation I walked over and pulled another chair up directly in front of the man. Honestly, his appearance was enough to scare most Christians into retreating to a safe zone. He had long, unwashed dark hair that was badly matted and dangling over his shoulders down to the middle of his back. He also had a long, dark unkempt beard that covered the majority of his facial features so that all you could see was his forehead, a small area of his cheeks, his nose and his eyes. Unafraid, I boldly sat down and introduced myself to him. At first he just kept repeatedly rocking back and forth muttering some unintelligible nonsense all the while keeping his head in a downward position. After only a couple of moments he finally raised his head and stared directly into my eyes. As soon as our eyes connected I realized why the counselors were so frightened. His eyes were violently vibrating back and forth as the darkness within him attempted to overwhelm me with the same fear that was choking out the faith of the counselors. Suddenly, a sound came out of him that was a low, guttural, other worldly voice proclaiming, 'I am Satan'. Normally this would have been enough to freak out even the most qualified counselors, but I had encountered this several times before ministering on the streets. By the grace of God, I was not the least bit frightened and simply waited a moment for him to realize I wasn't at all afraid. As his eyes continued to violently vibrate, I then said, 'I want you to know that I spent several years of my life serving Satan before I gave my life to Jesus. Therefore, I know him (Satan) very well. I don't mean to alarm you, but I have to be honest and tell you with absolute certainty that you are not Satan.' The disheveled man instantly slumped back in his chair and continued staring at me, but now he did so with a puzzled look of shock and unbelief. Suddenly, his sad looking eyes stopped vibrating and with a perfectly normal voice he asked, 'I'm really not Satan?' 'No, you are not', I replied. I then explained to him he was in fact deceived and was not who he thought he was, but could be exactly who God designed him to be if he received Jesus as His Lord and Savior. Tears began to flow from his eyes as he joyfully acknowledged he wanted Jesus to come into his heart and be the Lord and Master of his life. At that moment I turned back to the confounded (and much relieved) counselors and said, 'It's alright now. You can come and pray with him to receive Jesus into his heart.' After re-assuring the dazed and confused man he would be all right in the hands of the counselors, I returned to the stage rejoicing over the victory that had just been won in that man's life.

As I reflect back on this amazing experience I am reminded of the countless times I've encountered well-meaning believers who were engaged in trying to imitate some 'one' or some 'thing' they were never created or destined to be. When I first started in the ministry I was honored to be around some of the most powerfully anointed and well known people God has put on the earth to preach the gospel. One of those individuals was Rev. Jack Grey, a Methodist evangelist who was full of the Holy Spirit and bigger than life. Brother Jack had no fear and seemingly no boundaries he wouldn't cross when it came to telling others about Jesus. His boldness, passion and courage for sharing the Gospel resulted in a life that continually sought to do things I had never seen anyone else ever even think about. Not surprisingly, as a young minister I fell into the trap of imitating him rather than imitating his all consuming passion and love for God. I started talking the way he talked and preaching to others the same way he did. I became so much like him it wasn't long before I was no longer uniquely Jerry Williams, but instead had become a miniature Jack. After that summer with Brother Jack, I found myself floundering in my faith after arriving back at college. The Lord lovingly helped me understand how I had been imitating Jack so much he had become my focus, even though I loved Jesus with all my heart. I was trying to be like Jack more than trying to imitate what the Holy Spirit was doing in and through Jack.

Throughout the years I have had several instances wherein others who closely followed my life and ministry were attempting to imitate 'me' as a musician and psalmist of the Lord. Although that is deeply humbling, I know that in 'me' there is no good thing apart from what the Holy Spirit is accomplishing through me in Christ. Therefore, I have made it my goal in these situations to do all I can to help those who aspire to participate in the life and ministry God has worked in me to keep their eyes on the Lord Jesus, not me. When given the opportunity, I gladly commit to mentoring these individuals teaching them how to further become a vessel of the Holy Spirit bringing forth and accomplishing His will, not their own. I am truly honored that others see gifts in me they want to possess and imitate. Graciously He has anointed my life to bring glory and honor to

Himself through the music and message He alone has placed within my spirit, mind and heart. To God be all the glory and praise!

The Church today is plagued with a spirit of imitation that has weakened its resolve and polluted its purpose. I can't even begin to estimate how many people have approached me through the years saying, 'God has called me to do exactly what you are doing'. I am fully aware I am not the only psalmist God has raised up and anointed in my generation, but I am the only 'Jerry' He will ever create. We are all one of a kind creations of the Lord fearfully and wonderfully made for a unique and specific purpose. I'm not Jack Grey, David Wilkerson, Leonard Ravenhill, Keith Green, Dallas Holm, Carman or Andre Crouch. I am Jerry Williams, a psalmist, pastor, preacher, teacher and bond-servant of the Lord Jesus Christ. Do not misunderstand my point. The essence and end of Christianity is not to make a way for someone to 'fulfill all their desires' doing what they 'want' and living a blessed and happy life. We were created to bring glory and honor to God! He must be the One Who increases in and through our lives! We must decrease! How our lives ultimately bring Him glory and honor does not rest in our ability to imitate anyone else other than Jesus. On the contrary, it rests in our availability to His will being accomplished in and through our lives. Then and only then do we become vessels for His glory and praise in the earth.

If you are struggling finding your identity in Christ, then my prayer is you will begin to see yourself as He has created you. He has formed you for a God size purpose that has His greatness, glory and His DNA already uniquely embedded within you. As you see His greatness and purpose being displayed in others, be careful to not fall into the trap of desiring to be that person, but rather focus all your desire on imitating the attributes and characteristics of the One Who has shed His Own blood for your redemption and salvation. If you find you have spent years imitating those who are 'created', then simply repent and turn back to your loving

Creator. His promise to you is, 'I will restore the years the locust has eaten, says the Lord.' Frustration and failure is the diet of imitating others. Fulfillment is the continual feast of those who learn to imitate Christ. May you sit at table with Jesus today and hear Him speak your name to the heavenly host. In that moment you will once and for all know who you are in Him, and will never again struggle with the dangers of living your life with a 'mistaken identity'.

Prayer

Dear Father,

You said through Your prophet John, 'I must decrease! He must increase!' What good is it if I spend my life increasing in qualities and characteristics that belong to someone other than You? You are the Creator, Redeemer, Deliverer, Justifier, Propitiation, Prince of Peace and Savior of my soul. Who else is there that can stand and vie for my attention and allegiance who dares to compare themselves to You? Yet, in my haste I too often give my energy and devotion partially to others rather than wholly to You. Forgive me for spending so much time in unfruitful and frivolous endeavors pursuing the favor and acceptance of others. Increase my awareness and abilities to see and understand the height, depth, length and breadth of all You are. I fear my desire to be well liked and received by others has much to do with my wanderings into these seasons of imitating someone other than You. I know there have been times I 'performed' for men and their approval. Strip me from any and all need to find acceptance and approval from anyone other than You. Guard me from the pitfall of coveting some 'thing' others might possess rather than being content with those 'things' You have given me for my good and Your glory. Search my heart, O God, and see if there be any 'thing' within my heart that needs to be extracted. If so, then in Your grace and with all Your power tear out by the roots any and every 'thing' that doesn't have its origin in You. May You alone ever be my heart's desire. Amen.

The Story Behind the Song:

It was around 1993 and we were in the middle of performing a youth concert in the Seattle, Washington area. There were approximately 2,000 teenagers in the auditorium and the atmosphere was super charged with the presence and anointing of the Holy Spirit. The night had started aggressively with songs like *I Won't Be Denied*, *Let's Fight*, and *Give Them Back*. Suddenly, the Holy Spirit took over the concert as waves of Spirit breathed conviction fell on the entire gathering of youth. In a matter of moments, a holy hush blanketed the auditorium. The only sounds that could be heard in the midst of this holy visitation were young people throughout the building weeping and crying out to the Lord. By this time hundreds of teenagers had spontaneously flooded the front of the auditorium falling down on their faces crying out to the Lord. So many had come forward there was no more room available for hundreds of others who were also trying to make their way to the front. Being led by the Holy Spirit I invited those still coming forward to make their way onto the stage and stand with us. Within minutes the entire stage was covered with teenagers lying prostrate before the Lord weeping and worshipping at the same time. So many had pressed onto the stage I wasn't able to take a single step forward or backwards. For the next ninety minutes I stood playing my guitar and singing unto the Lord as hundreds of teenagers miraculously gave their lives to the Lord Jesus. At some point during this time of unhindered worship I began to spontaneously sing,

I wanna be more like You,
I wanna be more like You,
I wanna be more like Jesus with less of my weakness,
I wanna be more like You.

This simple little prayer caught fire in the hearts of the teenagers who then began singing it over and over as an anthem to the Lord. They continued singing this simple chorus for at least thirty minutes as the presence of God continued to dominate and overwhelm everyone in the auditorium. What a glorious memory and testimony to the birthing of this precious song. As you read through the words and possibly listen to the song may the Spirit of God overwhelm you as He did all of us in that auditorium in Seattle so many years ago.

PSALM 86 (I WANT TO BE MORE LIKE YOU)
(Song from the Warriors Arise project)
(Music and lyrics written by Jerry Williams)

Incline Your ear, O Lord for I am a needy man
Please let Your lovingkindness come and save me once again
Teach me all Your ways that I might know Your truth
Unite my heart to fear Your name that I might worship You!

<u>Chorus</u>
I want to be more like You. I want to be more like You.
I want to be more like Jesus with less of my weakness,
I want to be more like You.
I want to be more like You. I want to be more like You.
I want to be more like Jesus with less of my weakness,
I want to be more like You.

O Lord preserve my soul from these wicked, evil men
For You are great and merciful, deliver me from sin
Then Lord, with all my heart I'll glorify Your name
For there is no one else like You, You alone can save!

Chorus

DAY 25 A FATHER'S CONFESSION

And he will turn the hearts of the fathers to the children, and the hearts of the children to their fathers. Malachi 4:6

On September 1, 1970 at the age of twenty I committed my life to Jesus Christ as my Lord and Savior. I was so radically transformed by the Life of God now living in me I knew without any doubt I wanted to live the rest of my life serving my Savior and Lord. The months prior to my being saved I had become disillusioned and frustrated with my life which culminated in my walking away from a full scholarship and dropping out of college. Miraculously, within four months of giving my life to Christ the door opened for me to attend Oral Roberts University in Tulsa, Oklahoma. With a new hope for the future I arrived on campus the first week of January 1971. The Lord continued giving me amazing favor opening doors no man could open. In less than two weeks after arriving I was asked to sing for one of the chapel services that Rev. Roberts was speaking at. That was a miracle because everyone knew he never spoke without having 'The World Action Singers' do the special music. Soon after that morning chapel service I began receiving invitations to sing in revival meetings and churches all throughout the state. One such invitation came in early April when I was asked to be the special music for a large revival being held in Oklahoma City. Rev. Jack Grey, a Spirit filled Methodist minister from the Dallas, Texas area, was the guest evangelist. Rev. Jack was a powerful preacher whose words were so anointed they seemed to pierce the air and cut to the deepest part of your heart. I was so moved and challenged that first night I immediately made my way to the altar to pray. While crying out to the Lord I distinctly remember being burdened to ask for two specific things that at first made no sense to me. First, I asked the Lord to one day grant me the opportunity to learn what it meant to be a godly, loving husband. Secondly, and most surprisingly, I asked the Lord to one day grant me the opportunity to be a loving, godly father. I had no idea why I was so burdened to pray for those specific requests that night. The only thing I could imagine was maybe it had something to do with growing up never knowing my biological father, and never experiencing what it was like to be part of a godly family with a faithful husband and a loving father figure. What I do unmistakably remember from that night is hearing the voice of the Lord speaking to me saying, 'The day will come, My son, when the devil will try to destroy you through your children. Do not be afraid, I have overcome the enemy.' That 'word' was so REAL in that moment I actually wondered if I had heard the Lord's voice audibly. That night that 'word' was indelibly burned into my spirit, but I understood it was a 'word' for the future. Consequently, I simply tucked it away and pondered it in my heart never realizing how TRUE it would prove to be twenty years later.

Today I can unequivocally and joyfully testify that both of my requests made that first night of the revival nearly fifty years ago in Oklahoma City have been answered and fulfilled. I am the father of three adult children (two daughters) and the grandfather of six grandchildren (four girls). Without question some of the greatest joys I have experienced in my life have been directly due to the Lord answering those prayers and allowing me to become a husband and a father. At the same time, without question the deepest pain and darkest sorrow I could ever imagine experiencing have come into my life because I am a husband, father and grandfather. Had it not been for the 'word' the Lord so powerfully spoke into my heart at that altar so long ago, I do not believe I would have survived the unceasing onslaught of attacks the enemy has waged against me through the rebellion of my children and grandchildren. At first I was a steadfast and strong warrior of God, but as the war waged on year after year I slowly began to lose my confidence and hope. Eventually I became a casualty of the 'war' and momentarily quit the fight. Then one pitiful day I heard myself hopelessly whining to the Lord asking, 'How could this be?' I'm sure many of you have asked that same question a thousand times to the Lord. That's when the Lord once again reminded me of the 'word' He had spoken to my heart at that altar so long ago, 'The day will come, My son, when the devil will try to destroy you through your children. Do not be afraid, I have overcome the enemy'! Hallelujah! Suddenly the eyes of my heart were once again enlightened and the smothering darkness that had enshrouded my soul departed. Instantly I was once again filled with a holy courage and re-committed my heart to the promise of 'victory' God had given me so long ago FOR MY CHILDREN! I began thanking Him that, although I had made a million mistakes as a father and husband, I knew in my heart I had never taken for granted raising my children in the love, fear and admonition of the Lord. The Holy Spirit then greatly strengthened my heart assuring me He knew I had given each of my children the absolute best I knew how to give at that time. Instead of being overwhelmed with the memories of past failures, I was being flooded with memories of how passionate I had been in sharing with my children the precious nuggets of wisdom I had learned from the Holy Spirit along my journey. Oh, what wonderful memories of countless times I spent praying and proclaiming the promises of God's immutable Word over my children. Even now, all these many years later, I am still daily praying and proclaiming His promises over their lives. I am confident the day is coming when I will see with my own eyes the day of their salvation and our restoration as a loving family.

That doesn't mean there aren't still really hard days. On the contrary, I have had to learn how to check my emotions at the door every day. Otherwise, the momentary visible evidence of what I continue to see could easily 'steal, kill and destroy' my assurance and faith in the 'word' the Lord spoke to me so long ago. I can never deny that in my zeal and passion to be the best father I could possibly be I ignorantly made countless blunders along the way. The truth is every parent makes mistakes and blunders as they maneuver through the parenting stages. Still, the joys of the early years far outweigh all the wounds and disappointments of the latter years. Thankfully God's unconditional, sacrificial LOVE is an all-powerful force that overcomes, endures and bears all things. By the grace of God there are no longer any 'things' or any 'words' my children could ever do or say that have any possibility of destroying or diminishing my love for each of them. They will always be the physical answers to my hopeful and prophetic prayers so long ago at that altar in Oklahoma City. They are handpicked 'gifts' from God and my love for each of them is unconditional, and the devil cannot keep them without having a continual fight on his hands from me, a warrior of God. Just as they were handpicked to be my children, I was handpicked by the Lord to be their father and grandfather. A mistake many parents and grandparents make is believing that unconditional LOVE means all-condoning LOVE. TRUE UNCONDITIONAL LOVE will always refuse to condone, support or enable rebellion. LOVE gives you the courage to draw clear, God honoring lines, then WAIT upon the Lord to lead them to the TRUTH. Never forget that God didn't give you children for destruction, but handpicked them for His glory and praise.

I want to share something encouraging that happened during the summer of 2007. By this time it had been several painful years since we had heard from any of my children, but thankfully we had finally come to peace with all that was going on knowing God was still working in their lives and would one day bring them back to Him, and to us. Then early one morning we were unexpectedly contacted by my oldest daughter who shared that she wanted to bring the three grandkids and come for a visit. They were only three hours away and wanted to come immediately. You can only imagine our excitement as we were filled with hope this was the beginning of the restoration God had promised would come. They arrived the next day and we spent the following three days laughing, playing, eating and just hanging out doing fun normal family stuff. The second day I spent six hours playing in the pool with the grandkids which didn't bother me at all, even though it took several days after they left to fully recuperate physically. All the pain of so many wasted years was instantly washed away by their arrival. The morning they all left my daughter said the greatest words she could have ever spoken to me as her father, *I love you, Dad.*

A few days after my oldest daughter had visited we then received another unexpected invitation from my youngest daughter to come and visit her and her husband in Indiana. She had married a young Japanese man she met in college, then moved to Japan after graduating. They had lived in Japan for more than three years, but were now back in the states attending graduate school at Purdue University. I just so happened to be traveling in the upper Midwest when the invitation came which allowed me the opportunity to easily swing by to see them. Again, we were certain this was all the beginning of the promised restoration of our family, so our joy and expectation was overflowing. Initially I made plans to spend just one day with them not knowing exactly how the visit might go due to our strained relationship over the years. Honestly, I was a little hesitant to go by myself, but much to my joy we ended up having a wonderful day together doing things we had never done before as a family. She even cooked a meal for me, which was the first time she had ever cooked for her daddy. At the end of that first day my eyes filled with grateful tears of joy as she said to me, *Daddy, can you stay another day?* I joyfully replied, *YES!* After two more days I finally had to leave, but my heart was overflowing with joy because my little girl wanted to spend time with her daddy.

Sadly, those few days of hope and joy were short-lived and it's now been several years again since we've seen or heard from any of our children. By the grace of God we still have the precious memories and our confident hope that one day the *years the locust has eaten* will be restored. We still have days when our strength, hope and confidence are tried due to the years that pass without any communication. But whenever we feel ourselves growing weak in our faith, all it takes to be renewed is a moment in the presence of our faithful heavenly Father. He continually assures us He will never allow anything in our lives that is more than He knows we can bear, as long as we obediently walk in His footsteps following His commands. As an earthly father I would have never emotionally survived these past many years without Him at my side assuring me every step of the way. His grace and mercy have allowed me to triumph over the voice of my failures, flaws and enemies. Thankfully, because of Him my faith today is neither weakened nor tarnished, but remains steadfast in hope. I still believe He will one day 'restore the years the locust has eaten'.

In closing, I feel compelled to share one last thing with those of you who presently have strained or broken relationships with anyone you love, especially if it's with your children. First, do not overlook the fact that when you chose to sacrifice years of your life for the betterment and greater good of someone you love, you were imitating exactly what Christ did for us. Even Christ was rejected by those He loved and gave His Life for. True sacrificial living is directly born out of God's unconditional LOVE. So, don't be deceived into expecting those you sacrificed your best years for to do the same for you. It doesn't always work that way, but it also doesn't lessen the significance and value of your sacrifice in the presence of God. If your love, like Christ's, has been rejected time and time again, then rejoice that you have been counted worthy to share in the same sufferings He endured on our behalf. Also, be extremely careful you do not become emotionally and mentally hardened or embittered by the momentary rejection of those you love. Instead, run to the Lord and be instantly refreshed in His limitless LOVE that hopes all things, believes all things, and bears all things! Cast your burdens on Him, then let Him renew your faith, heal your heart and replenish your LOVE. Never be afraid to LOVE again, sacrifice again, and yes...even get wounded again by those you love. In the end LOVE will conquer ALL.

Possibly you are one of God's children who, like my children, have not communicated with your Heavenly Father in years. If so, then let me strongly encourage you to go back home to your Father. Can you hear His voice crying out to you right now, *I am here! Come unto Me and stay for awhile!?* If you will draw near to Him, then He will draw near to you. He loves you unconditionally and longs to spend time with you as His child. If you will do this, then I am certain He will hear you say, *Father, can You stay another day?*

Prayer

My gracious heavenly Father, You Who are the Father of all fathers and from Whom every family is named, I bow before You today as Your adopted son. I love and adore You for Who You are and sincerely thank You for all You've mercifully done for me. I am at a loss for words when I consider Your unconditional love toward me. Thank You for teaching me that Your righteous disciplines in my life are always birthed out of Your love for me rather than spawned out of disappointment or anger toward me. You are always faithfully there with an encouraging word of hope no matter how far I may have strayed in my ignorance, disobedience or blatant rebellion. Even in those seasons of severe discipline from Your hand I've always sensed Your unfading love and commitment toward me.

Thank You for answering my prayer and honoring me with the opportunity to be an earthly father. Thank You that the children You've entrusted to me were chosen to be a heritage unto You. I understand in Your choosing me for this honor You were fully aware of my character flaws and weaknesses. Yet, You still appointed me to bear the weight and responsibility for this holy calling. Therefore, I can confidently stand trusting that the destiny You've placed on my children is one of righteousness and holy service unto You. With that hope firmly entrenched in my heart, I beseech You to heal me from the deep wounds that have pierced the uttermost parts of my heart through the words and actions of my children. You most of all knew the afflictions that would shred my heart from the inevitable selfish, insensitive actions and words pouring forth from the lives of my precious God appointed children. How many times as Your child have I done the same things to You in my ignorance and selfishness?! Help me to continuously set my gaze forward in the hope and confidence the day is approaching wherein each of my children will wholeheartedly return to the 'way they should go' and fulfill their destiny which was formed in the workshop of Your love. Establish and solidify my heart in Your unconditional love and mercy that I might be to them all that You are to me.

O my Father, I understand that first and foremost You look upon the motive and intent of our heart. Alas, the performance of my destiny and duties as an earthly father didn't always follow the intentions of my heart. Too often my love was reactionary, shallow and conditional. Too often my disciplines were spontaneously exacted based on momentary disobedience rather than steadfastly flowing out of Your love for them. The guidance I offered too often came forth stern and sterile rather than encouraging and hopeful. Yet, knowing all this, my hope lies not in my shortcomings, but rather in Your infinite wisdom in choosing me to be their earthly father. Thankfully You have taught me that You never create something with a view of failure. Hallelujah! Therefore, my hope is secure and my belief unwavering that their future victory lies in the seeds of Your righteousness, seeds that were faithfully formed and sown out of Your heart and Word into their hearts when they were young. Therefore, O Father, hear the cry of this earthly father for my children today. Keep them which You have given me. Let the day hasten when their hearts are turned back to You as their heavenly Father. Restore the years the locusts have eaten and bring forth a harvest of righteousness from all the seeds sown in love, sacrifice and suffering.

I pray not only for my children, but for all those prodigals with seeds of destiny still yet to be birthed and manifested for Your glory and praise in the earth. Heal the shattered hearts of destitute parents who have fallen upon the altar of Your mercy and forgiveness. Renew their hope that one day soon You alone will revive and bring back all the sons and daughters destined for righteousness. It was not a mistake You chose us who made mistakes to be the conduits of children of destiny in the earth. May we see in this day a glorious returning of the hearts of our children to their parents. May we all one day victoriously stand together having finished the course prepared for us in the glory of Your presence. Amen. Amen.

Behold, children are a heritage from the LORD! Like arrows in the Hand of a warrior, so are the children of one's youth. Happy is the man who has his quiver full of them. They shall not be ashamed! Psalms 127:3-5

The Story Behind the Song

His Angels Are Everywhere is a song I wrote to my oldest daughter when she was just eleven years old. I can still see in my mind's eye her waving and crying as I would pull out leaving for another ministry tour. In those days touring was a part of the ministry that was unavoidable and required a sacrificial commitment on the part of everyone in the family. I always put on a happy face as I pulled away, never letting her see my tears once the tour bus was out of sight. This precious song was given to me by the Lord as a 'gift' to my little girl to help her in those times when Daddy was gone, but also to help Daddy know his little girl would be loved, guarded and protected until I returned home.

His Angels are Everywhere

(Song from the Give Them Back project, music and lyrics written by Jerry Williams)

Close your eyes child
See the stars dancin' till the morning light
And don't be afraid of the dark
His angels are everywhere

Dream of horses and candy land
You know your Daddy's bigger than the booger man
So ride out and chase the clouds
His angels are everywhere

Chorus
If the storm comes and you wake all alone
Lightning is flashing and Daddy is gone
Call out to Jesus and then you will see
The storm clouds roll away
Never believe what you hear in the night
Keep your eyes on Jesus and visions of light
Will come flooding over you

Close your eyes child
And make believe your teddy bear's alive tonight
And remember when the giants come
His angels are everywhere

O, what a feeling to be so free
Racing with the wind and the bumblebee
Flying high so you can see
His angels are everywhere

Chorus

DAY 26 HELPLESS HOLIDAYS

God is our refuge and strength, a very present help in trouble.
Psalms 46:1

All of our personal friends and family know that Christmas is hands down our favorite time of the year. Setting aside an entire season for the singular purpose of thanking God for the Gift of His Son is a time we excitedly look forward to every year. We've never been bothered or disillusioned by all the other hyper promotional 'stuff' that goes along with the season. On the contrary, we so look forward to Christmas each year it's not unusual for us to get started decorating before Thanksgiving. Our goal every Christmas is simple: make certain anyone who visits our home during the holidays feels as though they have entered into a winter wonderland wholly dedicated to honoring the Child Who came to take away the sins of all men. Honestly, there's almost nothing that can dampen or hinder our resolve to celebrate Jesus during the Christmas holidays. However, there have been a couple of years wherein unexpected circumstances momentarily opened the flood gates to all kinds of difficulties forcing us to reluctantly set aside our seasonal celebrations. The following is a story of one of those unexpected interruptions that tried to steal, kill and destroy our love of Christmas.

It was December of 1981 when we were living in Bloomington, Indiana. At the time we were a young family with three small children, and I was the associate pastor of a newly formed church in town. It had been several years since I had been able to return home to Texas for the holidays to see my mother, so we had been asking the Lord to somehow make it financially possible for us all to have Christmas that year at Granny's house. Our youngest daughter's first birthday was happening on the 19th, so we were really hoping to celebrate two birthdays that year with Granny. Although we loved the church where I served, the salary I was making made it impossible to consider taking such a long trip. One of the families in our church gave us a love offering for the holidays which unexpectedly gave us the funds to make the trip. Hallelujah! The drive from where we lived in Indiana to West Texas was normally a hard two-day trip, but the baby wasn't feeling well when we started out, so it ended up taking us three long days to finally arrive.

Before I continue with the rest of the story you need to understand that my childhood memories of the holidays with my extended family doesn't conjure up warm and fuzzy thoughts of making snowmen in the pure white snow, drinking hot apple cider and waking up each morning to the mouth-watering smells of homemade cinnamon rolls baking in the oven. On the contrary, we entered the holidays each year wondering if this would be the year we would actually make it through one meal without the family erupting in some ridiculous emotionally charged war of words. Our family was a mess and fully dysfunctional long before they started commonly using the word. There were several relatives that could hardly tolerate each other, so more often than not the atmosphere was awkward and intense. The commonplace war of words would usually break out among the opposite sides of the family over nothing more than who sat where at the table. Of course, this was never an issue with the kids who usually stayed outside playing, but at the same time kept waiting to see when the fireworks might begin. Consequently, I have far too many memories of Granny latching onto my hand and dragging me out the door as she angrily departed the family gathering. All these negative memories came rushing back in as we made the three-day journey westward. It doesn't take a rocket scientist to understand why I was on high alert by the time we arrived knowing we were going to see many of the same relatives that caused all those issues throughout my childhood years. By the grace of God that part of the trip went remarkably well and our visit with the family was an unexpected blessing.

Once we finally arrived at Granny's house, instead of being able to relax and finally enjoy the holidays, things took an unexpected turn for the worse with the baby. Like an unannounced tsunami, in a matter of just a few hours her fever spiked skyrocketing to 104. I hardly had time to even pray before we were racing her to the emergency room at the Medical Center Hospital in Odessa, Texas. It seemed like only moments had passed when the doctor came out to inform us she was dangerously dehydrated and in serious trouble. Things went from bad to almost frantic as her symptoms continued to rapidly plummet. It was like getting caught in a horror movie and we were the main victims. I still have vivid memories of helplessly staring out the window in her hospital room not knowing if she would survive the night. I was physically and emotionally exhausted stunned by the whole ordeal as I stood motionless watching her from the reflection in the window. The doctors had given us no real hope or assurance, but left us with nothing more than the grim possibility she might die before the sun came up. How could this be happening? We weren't supposed to be in the hospital! We were supposed to be opening presents while drinking hot cider and eating Christmas cookies and homemade pecan pie. I didn't make a sound, but quietly stood there crying out to God in my spirit. *God, where are You? Why don't You intervene and make this all go away? Please! Please! Please come and give me some hope You are here in this room with us!* At that moment the presence of God filled the small room and an overwhelming peace settled in my heart and mind. Nothing in the natural had changed, but God's presence was now permeating every square inch of the room. No one else consciously sensed His being there, but somehow I knew

He was telling me to not be afraid. In that instant I knew in my heart she was going to live and not die. Still motionless and quiet, I immediately made an altar to the Lord acknowledging again this baby was not mine, but wholly belonged to Him. I had done exactly the same thing several years earlier when our oldest daughter was in the hospital in Nashville, Tennessee with very similar symptoms and the same diagnosis. It's hard to explain, but I was suddenly overwhelmed with a God-sent calmness and knew in my heart she was going to be fine. This was not me trying to muster up enough hope to say things were going to get better. This was a direct 'word from God' released in my spirit and embraced with a heart of assurance and faith. In those few moments it was as though the Lord gave me a glimpse into the days appointed for this little girl who had been dedicated to Him while she was still in the womb. Within minutes her symptoms drastically began to improve and to the amazement of the hospital staff, we took her home the next day.

I don't remember much about our drive back to Indiana a few days later, but our lives had been forever altered by the events of that holiday season. That wasn't the last time I stood staring out a window asking God to intervene on her behalf. There have been many other holidays wherein I felt helpless to do what was needed to bring Light in the midst of darkness. Thankfully I have a Father Who is able to do exceeding abundantly more than I could ever ask or imagine. I guess that's why the holidays have become such a wonderful and special time for us. As I reflect on all the past blessings God has bestowed upon our lives I am overwhelmed by His infinite love and mercy. I am far too easily held hostage by the moment forgetting the bountiful blessings He has continually poured out for us over the years. As I look back on those years and all the amazing benefits He has showered down on my life, I can come to no other conclusion but this: God loves me so much He sent His only begotten Son to save me. Celebrating Jesus at Christmastime is my way of telling everyone I meet how much God loves me, and will forever be FOR ME. With

Him lovingly on my side, it doesn't matter what comes against me in this life. In Christ – I WIN!

This is just one of dozens of stories I could have shared concerning difficult times that have stormed in and out of my life, especially around Christmastime. Of all the lessons learned, the most valuable is without doubt this: whenever the unexpected storms of life come in like a flood, my faith and confidence must be firmly centered 'on' my 'Deliverer', rather than 'in' my 'deliverance'. Otherwise, should my certain rescue not come as speedily as I think it should, I may lose hope and quit running altogether. However, if my hope is established in Him rather than His help, I will always find strength and encouragement knowing He is right there with me. 'God is our refuge and Strength, a very present help in times of trouble.'

Are you going through a life storm right now? Are you feeling helpless with no idea what to do next? If you are struggling or even fainting in your walk with God? Then do your best to push away all the noise and confusion, and forcefully make yourself set your mind and heart on Christ alone. He Who cannot lie has promised to never leave or forsake you. Be assured in your hour of trial He is still with you. If He is with you (and He is according to His promise), then know in your heart of hearts that whatever is presently coming against you cannot conquer you or His purpose for you. Rise up! Encourage yourself today in the Lord! Lift up your eyes to the heavens and see the Lord of lords ever interceding on your behalf. Awake, O sleeper and arise from the dust. Put on the whole armor of God and stand. You need not fight in this battle for the battle is the Lord's, not yours. You are a child of the King of kings. If God is for you, then what does it matter who or what may be coming against you? This is the day the Lord has made. Make an altar to the Lord and choose to rejoice and be glad in Him!

Remember, living a Christian life doesn't mean freedom from all pain or tribulation. On the contrary, I'm here to assure you that you will most certainly at some point experience pain, struggles and difficulties in this life. However, I am also here to assure you that if you belong to the Lord, then 'no weapon formed against you can prosper'. The object of our faith is not trying to acquire and live a life free from all difficulties. The Object of our faith is living for the glory of the One Who gave Himself freely for our salvation and deliverance. For me, to live is Christ, and to die is gain!

Prayer

Heavenly Father,

In this hour of unceasing and relentless struggle, I am being compelled like Elijah to run away in fear. Help me to rest in the truth that You have numbered my days, and decreed that nothing shall confront me I am unable to bear, but with every temptation You will always provide an open doorway of escape. Oh my heavenly Father, give me the wisdom and courage to willingly accept the escape route You've designed and provided rather than unwisely place my hope and trust in someone else's plan. The cries of king David have become my daily mantra: How they have increased who trouble me! Many are they who rise up against me. (Psalm 3:1) I acknowledge, O Lord, my constant tendencies to focus on the trouble rather than keep my gaze securely on You and Your assured triumph. Teach me how to encourage my spirit in the promises You've supplied to me in Your unchangeable Word. Help me in the midst of this wicked deluge to proclaim as king David did, 'You, O Lord, are a shield for me, My glory and the One Who lifts my head.' I beseech You, O Father, deliver me from the snare the enemy has secretly laid to ambush me in my weakness. Rescue me from the intentions of self-promoting men who have designs on my harm for their personal gain. Anoint me with the gift of faith and drive out my fear in this dark and ominous hour.

Your promises and Your presence are all I desire and need for certain victory and vindication over my foes. I wish no harm on my brethren who have spoken words against me without permission from Your blessed Holy Spirit. Father forgive them. I understand they have acted in ignorance and do not know the dangers that lie ahead because of their deadly words and actions. As for the giants that have entered the land of my soul, help me rise up with the courage of Caleb and in Your might strike down all the sons of Anakim who block the way you have chosen for my life. Cover me with the blanket of peace that I might lie down and sleep in confidence fully assured that 'no weapon formed against me will prosper'. Thank You, Father. Thank You, Jesus. Thank You, Holy Spirit. Amen.

The Story Behind the Song:

Throughout the years I spent touring there were many days on the road that were a real challenge physically, mentally, financially and spiritually. Oftentimes these challenges were due to the personal issues erupting in the different members of the team/band. It was amazing how the attitudes of the different team members could change in a matter of hours causing the focus and unity of the team to be drastically altered. On the night I wrote *You Never Change* we were in High Point, NC and had just finished another concert. Although the Lord had blessed the night and people seemed to love what took place, I knew we were not at our best mentally or spiritually. As the team was breaking down the equipment I made my way to a back room of the auditorium to reflect and pray. While in that room the Lord powerfully met me assuring me He NEVER CHANGES, even though we are constantly changing. He gave me peace to trust Him with the members of the band and know that they were there because He placed them there, not because I chose them. Hallelujah! I picked up my guitar and began writing, and by the time the equipment was loaded I had written *You Never Change*.

<u>You Never Change</u>
(Song from the Holy Fire project)
(Music and lyrics written by Jerry Williams)

So many times in my life I thought it was You,
But I was mistaken
So many things in my life I thought were from You,
But now they've been taken

Chorus 1
But through the confusion and the times of defeat
And the struggle that always remains
No matter how hopeless and dark it may seem
You never change!

So many times in my life things that I've said
Were better unspoken
So many times in my life promises made
Lie shattered and broken

Chorus 2
But through all the seasons, the years of my life
One thing forever remains
No matter the struggle, heartache or strife
You never change!

So many times in my life decisions I've made
Seemed right at the moment
So many times in my life when I've run away
I've stumbled and fallen

But You never change!

DAY 27 A COLD NIGHT IN NORTH CAROLINA

Behold, I give you the authority to trample on serpents and scorpions, and over all the power of the enemy, and nothing shall by any means hurt you. Nevertheless, do not rejoice in this, that the demons are subject to you, but rather rejoice because your names are written in heaven. Luke 10:19-20

It was early spring and we had just arrived in Franklin, North Carolina for a city wide concert later that evening at the High School. Several months earlier a concerned group of Christian businessmen from that area had contacted us asking if we could come and do an outreach for the teens of their community. They had heard how God was moving through our concerts, and after much prayer invited us to come. Their plan was to launch a multi-week series of outreaches in their region using our concert as the catalyst for the events to follow. They had been praying for months prior to our arrival asking the Lord for a powerful outpouring of His Holy Spirit that would specifically impact the teenagers of their city and turn the tide of wickedness that was so rampant in the schools. By the grace of God their prayers were gloriously answered as we had an unprecedented outbreak of the Holy Spirit witnessing more than one hundred teenagers committing their lives to Christ at the end of the concert. Hallelujah! The following is a story about one of those tormented teens whose life was transformed the night of our concert.

Moments after the concert had officially ended I was still on stage speaking with what soon became a small mob of teenagers who had all visibly been moved by the Holy Spirit, but for some reason didn't come forward during the altar call. It's amazing how many times I have had the privilege to lead someone to Christ simply by hanging out afterwards and being available to talk. While I was still speaking with the ever growing throng of teenagers on stage, I was suddenly interrupted by an eerily cold blast of air that came sweeping over me from behind. I quickly discerned this wasn't simply the A/C cranking up on stage, but was in fact a coldness that was anything but normal or natural. As I spun around to identify where the source of this mysterious cold air was coming from, I saw a young teenage girl rapidly exiting the stage area. The Holy Spirit immediately confirmed in my spirit she was the source through which the strange coldness was emanating.

As I set my gaze on her, by the Spirit of God I knew this precious young girl was possessed and controlled by a demonic spirit. I immediately stretched out my hand toward her and loudly proclaimed the blood of Jesus over her life, rebuking the demon that possessed and controlled her. My hope was that she would turn around and come back to receive Christ, but as soon as I proclaimed the blood of Jesus over her, she slipped out the back of the auditorium and was gone. I stopped for another moment and prayed for her, then resumed my conversations with those on stage who were still wanting to hang out, talk or pray together. It couldn't have been more than fifteen minutes later when one of the young men on our ministry team approached me with a very concerned look on his face. 'Brother Jerry, a few moments ago we had a young teenage girl come up to us asking for prayer. Before we could begin praying over her she began to, well, it's hard to explain. We just need you to come and see for yourself. Her eyes are literally vibrating in her head and she is talking to demons!' Hoping it was the young girl I had prayed the blood over I quickly told those on stage I would return soon, then expectantly went with our young team member to the nearby dressing room. As I entered I first saw there were four of our other team members in the room, and they were all helplessly trying to pray for the tormented young girl. I then looked at the young teenager who was the source of all the confusion, and to my joy it was the very same young girl I had proclaimed the blood of Jesus over a few minutes earlier. She was sitting in a chair calmly carrying on an open conversation with some of the demons who had taken possession of her life and were now visibly manifesting to her in the room. And yes, her eyes were literally vibrating at a remarkably high speed as she spoke with the demons. The room was also filled with a dark, ominous presence of hell which had already overwhelmed our four young team members who had never seen or heard anything like this before. They were literally paralyzed with fear and totally confused. Without hesitation I slid a chair directly in front of the young girl and began to calmly, but boldly speak directly to her. The demons tried to control and dominate the conversation, but I quickly exercised the authority Jesus has given me as His ambassador and commanded the demons to be silent. Within a few moments the young girl's eyes completely stopped vibrating and she looked into my eyes finally acknowledging me for the first time. I then began confidently speaking the word of God over her life taking authority over the strongholds of hell who had gained access and control of her mind, body and spirit. Within minutes she was gloriously set free and called out to Jesus to save her soul. What a glorious sight to see her weeping with joy over the reality of the new LIFE within her. At that moment I turned back to the young, and completely astonished team members and instructed them to finish ministering the Word to our new sister.

What a glorious and awesome God we serve! We later discovered this young girl had been institutionalized for the past few years for killing a man who had been her psychiatrist. Her parents had been violently murdered several years earlier and following that horrific event she had been continuously terrorized by the forces of darkness and hell. Having no church home, she eventually yielded her heart and mind completely to the influence and control of the voices in her head. She was had been released from the psychiatric hospital (they had done all they knew to do for her) just a few days before we arrived, and by the grace of God met someone who told her about the concert. Amazingly she decided to come. After arriving at the concert the demons within her became tormented by the manifest presence of God filling the auditorium. She had been controlled so long by these demons she had actually given them personal names and spoke with them continuously. None of us knew anything of the WAR that was raging within her that night, but by the grace of God she refused to leave choosing rather to stay until the end. She desperately wanted to go forward during the altar call, but was too afraid. Therefore, when she saw I had stayed on stage afterwards, she decided to come forward to speak with me. Just before she reached me she was overcome with fear and bolted out of the auditorium. That's the moment I felt the mysterious demonically infused blast of cold air. However, on her way out of the auditorium she suddenly felt a strength and determination to turn around. She did just that, but this time, instead of trying to reach out to me personally, she sought out one of the younger team members who had been introduced during the concert. They in turn led her to the dressing room where everything else transpired. By the grace of God the last report we heard concerning this precious young girl was that she was going to church and growing in the Lord. Praise the Lord.

The Son of God Appeared for this purpose, that He might Destroy the works of the devil.
1 John 3:8

Prayer

My dear heavenly Father, I humbly and gladly acknowledge my life belongs to You and no other. You are the Master and Commander, the Lord and King of my life. Teach and train me to be a faithful and victorious warrior of Christ for Your glory. As Your servant, son and soldier it is my greatest honor and privilege to offer my life in service to Your purpose among men. Though once I was blinded by the glittering fool's gold of selfish ambitions, You have mercifully delivered me and opened my eyes to see how my brethren are being taken captive by the same spirit that once prevailed in my life - the lust of the eyes, the lust of the flesh, and the boastful pride of life. Give me favor in their presence as one who has been delivered and now points the way to victory and freedom rather than pointing the finger at their weakness and sin. I long to be a vessel of noble use in Your hand sent forth in the anointing that breaks off all the wicked chains of delusion and oppression that have entangled their hearts and deceived their minds.

Here am I, Lord! Send me forth to drive out the enemy who has stolen the confidence and sullied the godly character of so many of Your leaders in the Church. I ask for no undue honor or recognition from them, nor do I seek the easier path. I do have this request, that You would continually protect me from the pitfalls that come from the momentary praise of men. May I not be distracted by any personal desire to be 'accepted' by those to whom You are sending me. May my sufficiency be in simply knowing I have been ordained and anointed by Your Spirit to do Your bidding in a time such as this. I am fully aware of the dangers that lurk in the fading splendor of the delicacies of this world. Keep me ever mindful of Your purpose in my life that I may not stumble or wander away from the task You have commissioned me to carry out. Blessed Holy Spirit, I call on You to be the Strength of my heart and the constant Sustainer of my soul. Through Your power and anointing alone can I ever hope to fully complete this God ordained mission. Enable me to accomplish Your will that in the end I may be known in hell as a man of God! Amen.

The Story Behind the Song:

I remember well the day the Lord gave me the inspiration for the song *I Won't Be Denied*. We were attending our home church in Tyler, TX enjoying the presence of God, as well as some much needed down time from touring. As the pastor was preaching he suddenly began to boldly proclaim, 'I won't be denied! I won't be denied!' To this day I can't remember at all what the message was about, but the moment he began shouting those words the Lord began to download the lyrics for the song into my spirit. I reached over and grabbed the clip board used for visitors to sign if they desired more information concerning the church. I turned the paper over and started writing what soon became the chorus to the song. I became so excited knowing this was one of those 'God songs', the minute church dismissed I headed straight home to my studio and finished writing the song that afternoon. What a joy it was later that year when I was able to actually hold a concert in our home church and open with the song that was inspired through the preaching of our pastor. Thank You, Jesus. Thank you, pastor Jim.

I Won't Be Denied

(Song from the Mighty River project, music and lyrics written by Jerry Williams)

Trouble's on the rise, I can hear within my mind
A voice that keeps saying, 'You're going to die!'
So many times all I did was run and hide
Just kept on praying I wouldn't die

For too many years all I had was doubt and fear
And no understanding that I could be free
And so many tears thought I'd always have to feel
Like I was abandoned I couldn't see

Then a light from heaven came
And it opened up my heart to see
Then I heard a Voice that said,

'I have come that you might be free, free indeed!'

Chorus
I won't be denied! Gonna take my stand and fight
In the name of Jesus Christ!
I won't be denied! Gonna take my stand and fight
In the name of Jesus Christ!

Living on the run never seems to take too much
To get our attention but we never learn
Jesus, I can hear Him calling us to freedom
Gonna say, 'No more!' Not gonna bow my knee again
Not gonna be a slave to all this trouble and pain
Gonna say, 'No more!' Not gonna be defeated
By running away never again

Then a light from heaven came and it opened up my heart to see
Then I heard a Voice that said, 'I have come that you might be free, free indeed!'

Chant
I won't be denied I'm standing in the name of Jesus Christ! X2

Chorus

DAY 28 NO WEAPON FORMED AGAINST YOU

Warning: The following story may contain information that could possibly challenge some of the things you have always believed. The accounts listed in this story are absolutely true and have not been altered or embellished to enhance the story in any way. Should you choose to go forward you risk being stretched in your belief and stirred up in your faith to trust God to do the impossible through your life in the days to come.

For the word of God is living and powerful, and sharper than any two-edged sword, piercing even to the division of soul and spirit, and of joints and marrow, and is a discerner of the thoughts and intents of the heart. Hebrews 4:12

It was the spring of 1979 and I was still officially part of the pastoral staff of Evangelical Community Church in Bloomington, Indiana. During the school year this otherwise sleepy midsize town is transformed into a thriving, bustling community as thousands of students from all over the world converge upon the city to attend Indiana University. This annual global convergence uniquely creates countless opportunities to interact with students who have embraced a multiplicity of liberal ideas, faiths and lifestyles making the whole region a fertile ground for outreach and ministry. I moved my family to Bloomington in January of 1977 and in the first two years saw hundreds of students commit their lives to Jesus Christ as their Lord and Savior. This influx of new believers started occurring within the first few weeks of our arrival which led me to pioneer what we called 'Leadership

Families'. These were forerunners of what is commonly referred to as 'Life or Cell Groups' today. The main difference was the 'families' we birthed were intently focused on raising up radically committed disciples. Consequently, the Word of God, worship and prayer were the primary focus of each gathering, not fellowship and fun. Each week as we assembled it was understood there would be a built in flexibility to allow for a spontaneous move of the Holy Spirit among us. In no way did this mean we weren't prepared to teach each and every week. On the contrary, everyone attending had scriptural 'homework' to complete each week as well as designated scriptures to memorize. Another unique aspect of each 'family' was the opportunity every active member had to bring guests to the meetings. This was one form of outreach we encouraged each member to embrace. These 'guests' were never the focus of our meetings, and were embraced with open arms as we unapologetically worshipped our King Jesus. The following is a story about what happened in the life of one of those 'guests'.

It was a beautiful Spring evening and the members of the 'family' were arriving early as usual. People were hugging and joyfully talking with each other getting caught up on all the news of the week when unexpectedly a young man I had been reaching out to on the campus surprised us all by showing up as my personal guest. The reason none of us were expecting him was because he was a well-known, highly polarizing leading voice for the 'gay rights' movement on campus. Bill (name changed for privacy) was extremely extroverted and entered our 'family meeting' in his normal flamboyant manner. To be honest everything he did was excessively brazen, bold and flamboyant. Bill was always an unavoidable presence wherever he went as he continuously exuded feminine gestures and qualities that extended far beyond normal boundaries. This kind of behavior is commonplace in today's society, but in the late 1970's it was something you rarely encountered and was at the very least a shock to most people. As a result most of the Christians I knew (including most of those in the 'family') were openly uncomfortable around Bill, and I have to say even intimidated by the aggressive boldness he exhibited. Consequently, they found it easier to simply avoid him, which sadly was something to which he had become accustomed. I had seen this scenario several years earlier when I became friends with a very talented young man in the music department of our local Junior College. That young man who I befriended in college was a carbon copy of Bill, so the extroverted entrance didn't bother me at all. Instead, I quickly made my way to him and joyfully welcomed him as my honored guest into our 'family' gathering that night.

As was always our custom we opened the meeting with a time of worship. Then, after a few moments of corporate prayer, I would bring a teaching from the Word challenging and stretching the 'family' to go higher and further in their walk with the Lord. By the grace of God that particular night the anointing of the Holy Spirit came forth in an especially powerful way as the Word went forth. Scriptures spontaneously flowed out of my spirit as I taught from the living Word of God. It wasn't long before there was a Spirit breathed electricity pulsating through the entire room as the manifest presence of the Lord filled the house. Everyone in attendance became so energized in the supernaturally charged atmosphere I continued teaching well past the usual allotted time. Finally, after almost two hours and many shouts of joy I sensed it was time to close the meeting with prayer. As soon as the 'Amen' was voiced and people began to disperse, Bill made a beeline directly for me. This time, however, he was not flaunting his normally bold and brazen attitude, but was instead visibly troubled in his heart and mind. As I reached out my hand to thank him for coming he asked, *Will you pray with me?* All evening I had watched him wrestling with the Truth of God's Word and the conviction of the Holy Spirit. Now he was face to face with the darkness in his soul and the marvelous Light that is Jesus Christ. Excitedly I gathered six of the younger brothers from the 'family' to accompany me to another area in the house to pray for Bill without distraction. Whenever I sense there may be deliverance involved I usually move the person to a place of privacy to eliminate any opportunity for confusion. The devil loves an audience and will do anything possible to gain control of a meeting through wild displays and demonic manifestations that quickly become the 'center of attention'. When this happens the thoughts of those present are easily drawn away from the Lord and their focus is turned to men rather than the Prince of Peace. Knowing this I was able to find a large room toward the back of the enormous home where I then placed a chair in the center of the room and asked Bill to take a seat so we could gather around him and pray. What took place next was one of the most unusual spectacles I have ever witnessed and something none of the eight individuals in that room would ever deny and will certainly never forget.

Before I reveal what took place next let me acknowledge that I am well aware many of our most influential churches in the West do not believe demons exist or that miracles still take place in the earth today. How they choose to ignore the obvious is baffling to me, especially when I have personally encountered both demons and seen thousands of documented miracles in my lifetime. Demons do exist and God is still doing miracles. How anyone can go through the motions of worshipping a God they proclaim to be ALL MIGHTY and ALL POWERFUL, then never BELIEVE Him to MOVE in POWER in our midst doing things we cannot ever hope to accomplish is ludicrous to me. NOTHING is impossible for the Lord Who is the same yesterday, today and forever!

Now for the rest of the story. The moment Bill sat down in the chair he immediately leaned forward in a state of brokenness placing his face in his hands. Then within less than ten seconds strange noises began to come forth from his voice and his physical appearance began to visibly transform. As he slowly raised his head a voice came out of him that was not of this world saying, *You can't have him! He's mine!* I was undaunted by this development since I had seen and heard this many times in the past. However, the six young brothers I had taken in the room with me were instantly overcome with fear which quickly paralyzed their faith.

What physically manifested over the next several minutes sent a shock wave through the hearts of those six young disciples causing them to literally back up until their backs were pressed against the interior wall of the room. Bill's facial features began to literally transform and his physical appearance began to take on another shape. His cheek bones began to protrude, his jaw became extended, his eyes became little more than widened slits in his face, the color of his facial skin began to darken and the demonic voice emerging from within him became more ominous, confident and threatening. All the while his shoulders, chest and back continued swelling until he looked more like a professional body builder rather than the effeminate young man who had arrived earlier for the meeting that night. The last and final phase of this demonic transformation occurred when the muscles in his arms and legs began to expand stretching the clothes he was wearing to the limit. Finally, the hideous transformation was complete and I was suddenly face to face with the physical manifestation of a demonically possessed human being. I had read accounts of this kind of physical transformation happening, but had never been an eyewitness to anything remotely like it. Honestly, had I not been there and personally witnessed this transformation myself, I probably wouldn't have ever believed it. But, I was there, it did happen, and to this day there are eight eye witnesses to all God did in the glorious moments following Bill's demonic transformation.

At this point a dark, suffocating evil presence began to overwhelm the very air in that little room. The demon within Bill began to boldly threaten to kill him as well as me if I didn't immediately cease every attempt to free him in Jesus' name. I quickly turned to the six terrified young men and strongly challenged them to start proclaiming the blood and name of the Lord Jesus and pray with all their might. By the grace of God even though they were literally trembling in fear, they began openly praying. Hallelujah! Within moments the Holy Spirit came in like a flood and the living Word of God began to flow out of my mouth as it had earlier that evening. I began boldly and triumphantly declaring freedom over Bill's spirit, soul, mind and body in the name of Jesus Christ.

Within a few minutes the glorious breakthrough came as I continued to relentlessly bombard the demon with the Word of God. Suddenly Bill violently threw his head back and let out a window shattering, bloodcurdling scream that unnaturally lasted somewhere between fifteen and twenty seconds. The moment he stopped screaming he slumped over in the chair and became completely motionless. As I knelt down beside him I quickly realized he wasn't breathing and there were no visible signs of life in him. As the six younger brothers drew near I could see exactly what they were thinking, *O Jesus! He's dead*! I immediately called all of them to join with me in once again pleading the blood of Jesus over him asking the Lord to raise him up and breathe the Breath of Life back into his lifeless body.

As we encircled his motionless body and continued crying out to God, something wonderfully strange and beautiful happened. Another loud and unusual sound filled the room. This time, though, the sound wasn't dark and ominous, but was much like what you would hear when airing up a flat tire. God was literally breathing LIFE back into Bill's lifeless body. We all watched with wonder and amazement as his body filled with the living Breath of God. At the same time all the demonically altered parts of his body quickly disappeared as the Breath of God poured into his lungs. This, too, lasted for about 20 seconds, but it seemed like a much longer amount of time to all of us standing there. When the sound finally stopped we were all greatly relieved to see him freely breathing again. Then he slowly lifted his head and with a look of complete astonishment spoke to me in a voice as normal as any man's saying, *Jerry?* Then he burst into tears of great joy as the power and love of Almighty God had completely transformed and set him free in the name of Jesus. At that moment all the brothers embraced him in tears rejoicing in all the Lord had done in each of our lives in that room that evening. Before we exited the room Bill completely renounced his gay lifestyle and fully surrendered his heart to the Lord Jesus as his Master, Savior and Lord.

As we returned to the main part of the house we were surprised to find that most of the 'family' had remained and were praying the entire time we were ministering to Bill. Within a year from that night Bill had married one of the young ladies who was part of the 'leadership family' and within five years of their wedding God had blessed them with three beautiful children. To God be the glory!

Most assuredly, I say to you, he who believes in Me, the works that I do he will do also; and greater works than these he will do, because I go to My Father. And whatever you ask in My name, that I will do, that the Father may be glorified in the Son. If you ask anything in My name, I will do it. John 14:12-14

There are millions of Bill's in our nation and world today who desperately need to encounter the power and presence of God. I pray God fills us all with a holy boldness that will motivate us to unashamedly rise up in this desperate hour and be those Spirit filled beacons of Hope and Truth to a world bound in darkness. I, for one, am weary with the impotent visions of a Church that has befriended the world rather than besieged it with the Sword of the Spirit and the glory of God's presence. Too long the accolades of the world have been laid at the feet of the leaders of the Church. It's time to once again repent and return with all our hearts to the Lord. If we, as His people, will humble ourselves and pray, turn from our wicked ways and seek His face, then possibly in His infinite mercy He will visit us again with signs and wonders that bring glory and praise to Him alone and will bring healing to our land. So be it, Lord!

For we do not wrestle against flesh and blood,
but against principalities, against powers,
against the rulers of the darkness
of this age, against spiritual hosts of wickedness
in the heavenly places.
Therefore, take up the whole armor of God,
that you may be able to withstand in the evil day,
and having done all, to stand.
Ephesians 6:12-13

Prayer

Heavenly Father,

You are truly awesome and amazing, and the wonders of Your handiwork are more magnificent and expansive than my finite understanding could ever hope to comprehend. Each time I witness Your power and love transforming a seemingly worthless and forgotten life into one of purpose, destiny and manifest joy, I am overwhelmed by the greatness of Your love, mercy, kindness, goodness and power. The height, depth, length and breadth of Your love is truly unsearchable and unmatched in all of creation. To consider that You have called me into Your service to be an ambassador of Your greatness, Your Life, Your love, Your Word and Your power is an honor that exceeds all accolades I could ever imagine being bestowed upon me by men. O God, please continue to help me never set my gaze upon the flaws and failures of others I encounter, but rather see them with Your eyes and respond to them with Your unconditional love and Life giving words. Help me to be a heavenly treasure hunter who joyfully looks past the putrid to find the precious. Give me the courage to launch out into the depths of someone's despair with the lifeline of Your hope. May my words be Your words, my thoughts Your thoughts, my actions only those 'works' You have prepared beforehand and ordained that I should walk in while living on this earth. Protect others from being distracted by the many flaws that still linger in my life. May Your reflection be the Light of my life that draws those men I meet along the journey to You. May I continue to increase in Your wisdom, knowledge, insight and discernment that I might give a 'word in season' to any and all I meet along the way. May I not grow weary with those who do not respond quickly to Your invitation to freedom and Life. Impart to me a tenacious spirit and a courageous heart that will never give up, never retreat, never say never, but always believes You for the impossible when the situation seems hopeless.

Lord lay some soul upon my heart, and love that soul through me
And may I humbly do my part to win that soul for Thee!

Lord, lead me to some soul in sin, and grant that I may be
Endued with power and love to win that soul, dear Lord, for Thee!

To win that soul for Thee alone will be my constant prayer,
That when I've reached the great white Throne I'll meet that dear one there.

Amen. Amen.

The Story Behind the Song:

It was the late 1970's and I had clearly heard the Lord calling me to take a step of faith and move forward with launching Harvest Ministries. At that time Contemporary Christian Music was still in its infancy and those of us who were called of God to be its pioneers were being challenged with huge sacrifices physically, spiritually, financially and relationally. As I wrestled with this prospective move, the Lord opened my eyes to the myriads of faithful men and women who in generations past had believed God through seemingly insurmountable situations and came forth victorious through *The Blood of the Lamb*, Jesus Christ. The mountains that stood in our way looked ominous and foreboding, but God kept telling me to FACE THE MOUNTAINS AND COMMAND THEM TO MOVE IN THE NAME OF JESUS! The words, 'they overcame him through the blood of the Lamb' kept resounding in my heart until I could do nothing else but move forward in faith fully assured I would OVERCOME by *The Blood of the Lamb*. At that point, writing the song *The Blood of the Lamb* was simply a byproduct of what the Lord had already done in my heart and spirit. Amazingly the song became a battle cry for countless believers in the years to come who began facing their personal mountains in faith and overcome by *The Blood of the Lamb*.

And they overcame him by the blood of the Lamb and by the word of their testimony, and they did not love their lives to the death.
Revelation 12:11

The Blood of the Lamb
(Song from the Send Us to the World, music and lyrics written by Jerry Williams)

I'm weakened by the raging war, standing when I feel no more
Like standing for the things that I believe.
Surrounded by the lives of men
Who stood when hope seemed at an end
Darkness all around, still I see.

The mountains moving in the night
Don't stand a chance to drag me down
'Cause I'm a mountain climber
I've learned the secret of those men
Who stared at death and conquered sin

And I'm gonna shout it from the mountains!

Chorus:
They overcame him through the blood of the Lamb!
They overcame him through the word that He'd said!
They overcame him through the name of
God's Own Son, Jesus Christ!
They overcame him through the blood and
The word and the name of Jesus Christ!

No matter how the days may go He said the war would never slow
Until that final day when Jesus comes.
So lift your eyes and gaze on Him, lay aside each weight of sin
Let your spirit soar where eagles fly.

The mountains moving in the night
Don't stand a chance to drag you down
'Cause you are now a mountain climber.
Spread your wings and catch the wind,
Stare at death and conquer sin
And shout it from the mountains

Chorus

DAY 29 KING OF THE MOUNTAIN

Assuredly, I say to you, unless you are converted and become as little children, you will by no means enter the kingdom of heaven. Therefore, whoever humbles himself as this little child is the greatest in the kingdom of heaven. Matthew 18:3-4

No matter where I travel I still find kids are intrinsically the same regardless of where they live geographically. These wonderful little people have some amazing built in qualities that catapult them directly past imminent danger straight to the playground of their imaginations. They ingeniously seem to always find creative ways to make an imaginary game out of every moment, no matter the environment or circumstance surrounding them. The next time you are in a crowded public place, purposefully dedicate a few moments to watch the children. It won't be long before you see those magical qualities at work transforming their otherwise chaotic surroundings into a mobile make-believe playground. Have you ever noticed how kids can instantaneously turn a mall or grocery store into a magical kingdom? That's probably the quality I love most when watching or spending time with these amazingly carefree little people. There really isn't any need to supply them with the latest and most expensive toys or high tech gadgets. All these remarkable little ones really and truly need is just a few minutes of uninterrupted freedom. Within seconds they're off on some new adventure slaying dragons or conquering the evil lords and rulers of the land. It takes no effort whatsoever for a child to enter a realm wherein their thoughts and actions are translated to a place where the impossible is commonplace. To them the world is just waiting to be discovered, and everything evil is there to be conquered.

That's why I find it especially interesting that Jesus said we must enter the kingdom of heaven *as a little child* (Luke 18:17). These words weren't spoken to the multitudes following Him at a distance, but were specific words that targeted His disciples. What was He saying to these radical followers that was best said by using the example of a little child? Can you remember the days when you first came to Christ and instantly believed in the impossible? That's precisely why it is so wonderful and exciting to have new converts in the church. They are constantly on the move looking for treasures that have yet to be discovered or enemies that must be conquered. They haven't yet 'learned' or been 'turned' by the example too often set by older believers who have long since embraced the idea that many of these things are no longer possible for the average Christian in an average church with an average expectancy for the days ahead. (Of course, I don't believe that either!)

I can easily remember my early days as a new believer. My heart was soaring with faith, expectancy and a God size imagination. I imagined a thousand great and mighty things God might do in and through my life. Oh how I dreamed and longed to make it to the top of the mountain and knock down any and all giants who would try and de-throne me from this incredible new Life I was now experiencing in Christ. Each day became an all-out race to lay hold of every prize and promise I could see in the living Word of God. Failure was never a consideration because faith was bursting out of every part of my being. When I would read that *nothing was impossible* for my heavenly Father, I simply believed it was the Truth and applied that confident belief to whatever I was facing that day. It's amazing how in those early days there was a continuous and contagious joy in my life that was much more spontaneous than most of my current days. Does this sound like something that might describe your life, too?

Somehow and somewhere along the way I became so consumed with growing up and 'doing' things for God I left behind the exhilarating joy of just knowing I was with HIM! Therefore, I have purposed in my heart to do whatever is necessary to return to those times with my heavenly Father where just being with HIM is more than enough. I am much older today, but still nothing brings my heavenly Father greater pleasure than when I come running to Him as His little boy. As an earthly father, there was nothing I loved more than when my kids would come running into the bedroom early in the morning and leap onto the bed to start the day playing. Within seconds we would turn the bed into a make believe fort or mountain. Other times I would get in the middle of the floor and they would all pile on top of me seeking to conquer the invading giant. Those were wonderfully joyful times that have regrettably long since been left behind.

It has been decades since the sounds of my kids running to daddy to play 'king of the mountain' have been heard in our home. All my children are now adults who have long since lost that sense of childlike interaction with their father. One day recently I was reflecting and praying about this when the Lord asked me, *My son, when was the last time you came running to Me leaping into My lap as a little child to start the morning?* I was astonished and ashamed when I realized I had ignorantly done the same thing with my heavenly Father that my children have done with me. In that moment I realized how much I had been neglecting that personal 'Father' time with the Lord. Don't misunderstand, I have consistently spent great amounts of time with my Father, but rather than running to Him with a joyful heart full of expectancy and God size imagination, I have continually run to Him with a thousand requests and a truck load of burdens. He has mercifully never turned me away, but just as I have missed those times with my grown up children, He was lovingly telling me how much He, too, has missed those personal 'Father – son' times with me.

The Word of God clearly teaches that *to whom much is given much is required.* As we grow older and more responsibilities are attached to our lives, we need to be especially careful to never allow the responsibilities to rob us of our opportunity to daily *come unto Him as a little child.* When we played king of the mountain in our home it was always much more fun when the whole family joined in rather than just one or two. I have a great idea today. I'm about to run in and jump into the lap of my awesome heavenly Father and spend a few moments playing 'king of the mountain' with Him. Don't worry, He always lets me win. Would you like to come along with me? I promise it will be a great time all together. Come on! Stop what you're doing for a few moments, get up and come with me. Our Father will love having us all there, and if we don't get in too big of a hurry we can all take turns being 'king of the mountain'. Father, ready or not here we come!

<u>Prayer</u>

My dear heavenly Father,

You alone are the Author and Giver of true and lasting joy. In this moment fill my weary heart with that inexpressible joy that comes only from being in Your presence. Please forgive me for not coming more often to simply spend time with You as my Father. I know I need You more than anything else, and I sincerely believe You are the first and foremost Love of my life. However, I still somehow get too busy trying to accomplish things for You rather than first coming and choosing to just be with You. Oh my heavenly Father, restore unto me the joy of my salvation! Create in me a new heart and mind that will never again allow the blessedness of doing things for You to supersede the decision to come unto You as a little child. Help me to never place performing before praising You. I fear I have allowed my heart and mind to believe the duties are my security rather than, like a little child, wholly trusting in You to supply everything I need for life and godliness. No child ever worries about what they will eat, drink or wear tomorrow. Therefore, I run to You today fully acknowledging that You alone are the Author and Fountain of Life, Love, Joy, Faith and Hope. Thank You, Father, for being so lovingly patient with me. I lay down my anxieties, fears, failures, shortcomings, desires and duties to tell You, I love You, Father! Thank You for adopting me to be Your son. Thank You for all You have provided for my welfare and sustenance through the years. Thank You for never leaving or forsaking me even though I have miserably failed time and again. Thank You for letting me know how much You amazingly want to spend time with me. Thank You for providing an open door wherein I can enter Your presence as often as I choose. Here I am now, Lord. I ask for no 'thing', but only come to be with You and hear Your voice. Thank You that You are here! Thank You that I am no longer an invited guest, but am now Your adopted and beloved son. That is more than my finite mind and heart can comprehend. I love You! Amen.

<u>The Story Behind the Song</u>:

Just a few months prior to writing *Know That I Am God,* I had taken a God size step of faith and moved my family and ministry to East Texas where we had no established relationships and no local support team. I set up my office in our detached two car garage because we couldn't afford anything else at the time. In those days, there were only three of us on staff, and all of us had to wait on the Lord each month to somehow, some way provide what we needed to feed our families. It was in the midst of these formative, lean months when the Lord literally spoke the lyrics to *Know That I Am God* into my spirit. The timing was perfect as I was struggling with anxiety and fear mostly concerning how to take care of the other families in the days ahead. As I began writing down the powerful promises God was speaking to my heart, Hope began to flood my spirit and dominate my thoughts once again. The music didn't take long to formulate as the 'word' was alive within my heart. As soon as I finished the song I distinctly remember excitedly going out into the office to share the newly formed song to the two other staff members. What an amazing and powerful time we all had in the presence of the Lord that afternoon. All worry and fear for the days ahead was eradicated and a new corporate resolve was ushered in through the anointing of the Holy Spirit. We were all united and keenly focused once again in a common purpose and call. Although we had each been through some difficult days and deep waters, this 'word' from the Lord brought a flood of reassurance that God was indeed leading and guiding us. With a renewed confidence that we were all still in the center of God's will, we set our faces like flint for the days ahead. Over the next decade we gloriously were anointed and led by the Holy Spirit to see tens of thousands come to Christ. To God be all the glory!

Know That I Am God

(Song from Voices, music and lyrics written by Jerry Williams)

Behold I lift My hand and set before you all My plans
To bring to every son of man Jesus Christ the Lord.
Behold I made you strong, I molded you a precious stone,
Then gave to you an everlasting song unto the Lord!

So, if in darkness you lose your way,
The river rises, don't be afraid.
I've walked the deepest part of every river that can rage.
When you're broken and all alone,
Your love has faded, your strength is gone,
Remember I gave My only Son that you might know.

Behold, the time has come to gather all My chosen ones,

Then separate them from the wicked sons who love this world.
Behold, I am the Lord! I stop the wind! I still the storm!
No weapon that is ever formed against you shall prevail.

So, if in darkness you lose your way,
The river rises, don't be afraid.
I've walked the deepest part of every river that can rage.
When you're broken and all alone,
Your love has faded, your strength is gone
Remember I gave My only Son that you might know -

The storms will come, the rains will fall,
But in your darkest hour of all,
Lift your eyes and know that I am God!

The storms will come, the rains will fall,
But in your darkest hour of all,
Lift your eyes and know that I am God!

DAY 30 BUMPUS MILLS, TENNESSEE

Now to Him Who is able to do exceedingly abundantly above all that we ask or think, according to the power that works in us, to Him be glory in the church by Christ Jesus to all generations, forever and ever. Amen. Ephesians 3:20-21

Oftentimes God's greatest designs in our lives start in small and obscure places. That's exactly what happened one Sunday morning in January of 1977. I had just entered the Middle School where the newly formed Evangelical Community Church (ECC) was temporarily holding their services. It was officially my first Sunday as the newest addition to the pastoral staff, and because I had arrived only two days earlier with my young family in tow I had no responsibilities other than showing up and being introduced to the congregation that day. Since I didn't have to preach, teach or lead in worship it was a perfect time to meet the people and get a feel for the flow and personality of the church. Soon after the service began a young graduate student from Indiana University was introduced as the special music for that morning. As he began singing I immediately took notice that his voice was strong and remarkably well trained. What grabbed my attention, though, was how skillfully he accompanied himself on a classical guitar. As I sat listening I felt an urgency to reach out to him knowing in my spirit this talented young man was merely performing a song about the Lord rather than offering a song of worship and praise to the Lord. By the time he finished his performance it was absolutely clear in my spirit this young musician had never personally met the One about Whom he had just sung. I somehow knew in my heart I was supposed to make every effort to share the Good News of a personal Savior with him. A few minutes later a unique opportunity was extended to every college student present to sign-up for a free home cooked meal the following week with one of the families of the church. What a great idea! Offering a home cooked meal to a college student was like setting a barrel of honey in front of a starving bear just coming out of hibernation. In that moment I knew a home cooked meal would be the perfect vehicle to try and connect with the young musician. After all, it was free food.

The next morning was my first official day in the office. After I was given the obligatory tour and shown my office space, I then politely asked Rita (the only secretary on staff who ran the church like a drill sergeant) if the young man who sang the day before was on the list for a home cooked meal. She checked and found that he had indeed signed up along with his roommate. I again politely asked Sergeant Rita if she would be so kind as to make sure they were both marked down to be at our home for their promised home cooked meal. She graciously obliged, and the invitations were sent out that day. Later that week Paul Wilbur (the young musician) arrived on schedule with his roommate, Ed Kerr, in tow. Right behind them were four other students we ended up inviting who had also signed up, but didn't have anywhere available to go. Needless to say it was a full house. Thankfully we had prepared plenty of food for everyone, but the heavenly food shared that day around our small, cramped dinner table has continued to impact lives for the Kingdom of God until this day. What God birthed around that obscure little table in January of 1977 has resulted in millions of lives being challenged, touched and impacted for Christ all over the world. None of us could have remotely imagined what God was about to release through that seemingly normal afternoon lunch gathering. I don't even remember what we ate that day, but what I do remember is how the Holy Spirit began to powerfully work in the hearts of each student present. During 'the Meal' I learned that Ed grew up the son of a Presbyterian pastor and was presently a graduate student at IU studying to be a classical concert pianist. It didn't take long to realize that even though he was a pastor's kid, he had never felt the need or conviction to commit his life to Jesus Christ as his personal Lord and Savior. That afternoon a chain reaction of God ordained events began to unfold that would soon culminate in Ed having a life changing personal encounter with Jesus Christ.

In the days following 'The Meal' Paul and I quickly bonded as friends. We discovered we had many similar things in common, but it was the music that became the common bond and vehicle through which I would mentor and challenge both he and Ed. I poured myself into teaching them how to seek to use their God given talents for His glory, something they had never considered. A few weeks later I launched a mid-week service completely geared to reaching and discipling students. This created a perfect venue to ask Paul and Ed if they would consider helping me form a student praise team. They both accepted the challenge and for the next several weeks I began teaching them the difference between performing songs about the Lord and actually singing songs TO the Lord. Once the meetings began they were radically impacted by the presence of God that was continually ushered in through our times of worship. Although neither of them had yet been born again, they were now consciously sensing and seeing how the Lord will inhabit our praise when it's offered to Him for His glory alone. It wasn't long after being in God's presence a few times that Ed came to my office one afternoon seeking counsel. He was wrestling with everything he was now experiencing and knew something had to dramatically change in his life. By the grace of God, I had the privilege of leading him to Christ and being an eye witness of his glorious transformation in Christ. For more than two hours he sobbed and cried out to the Lord for mercy and forgiveness as the Holy Spirit opened his eyes to see with clarity the depravity of his own heart and his desperate need for a

Savior. When he finally rose up from the floor of that office he was visibly changed and gloriously born again. Hallelujah!

It just so happened that the following weekend I had scheduled a weekend retreat out of state for all our youth ministry leadership. The retreat was not an outreach, but designed to be a consecrated time for me to meet and pray with the leadership team God was building at the student church. Now that Ed was radically saved I knew I needed to invite him to come. Because Paul was Ed's roommate, we decided to invite him to come along as well. Somehow I knew this wasn't going to be an ordinary weekend, but I had no idea God was putting something in motion that would ultimately touch the world. We arrived in Bumpus Mills, TN late Friday afternoon and quickly got settled in for our overnight retreat. After an early meal, we came together for a time of worship, teaching and fellowship. We all got up the next morning just after sunrise and met together for a precious time of worship and prayer. As we began singing the Lord's presence came in like a flood and the Holy Spirit literally took over. Soon afterwards I felt impressed by the Holy Spirit to send each person on a prayer walk in the woods. I gave them a full hour alone listening for God's voice to speak to their hearts. Those sixty minutes walking and praying in the woods impacted the lives of everyone on the team, but for Paul it was life changing. As he walked back into the meeting area it was obvious to everyone he was visibly different. Trembling, he began to express the amazing things that took place as he walked alone in the woods with His Creator. Once finding a quiet place only a few hundred yards from the cabin he decided to sit and take in the beautiful morning. Suddenly, he was startled as he heard footsteps right behind him. Swinging around to see who it was coming up behind him he saw only empty woods. Then the presence of the Lord swept through the area where he was sitting overwhelming every fiber of his being. Instantly he knew it was God Who was walking in the woods with him. He was so overwhelmed by His presence, he began to cry out to the Lord for mercy, forgiveness and salvation. That day in the woods outside Bumpus Mills, TN Paul Wilbur was gloriously saved and called into the ministry of the gospel of the Lord Jesus Christ. Thank God for small beginnings.

Now that both Ed and Paul were radically saved, the music at the student church took on a whole new anointing and power. Students began to flow into the meetings each week with dozens being saved each month. Within two years we were ministering in a five state region performing an average of two hundred worship concerts per year. It was then the elders at ECC approached us realizing the ministry God had birthed in us was bigger than ECC and needed to be taken to the world. By August of the next year we took a step of faith and launched Harvest, which soon became a forerunner of contemporary Christian music. The music of Harvest has gone throughout the world and is still impacting lives and being played around the globe today. Ed Kerr became a songwriter and worship teacher for Hosanna Integrity. Paul became a Messianic artist for Hosanna Integrity and has recordings in four languages which has now been distributed in more than eighty nations.

I can't explain it, but when I heard Paul singing on that brutally cold morning in January of 1977 something in my spirit was stirred. Somehow I knew we were destined to see the gifts God had given us touch many lives, but I had no idea God would use that small beginning to touch the world. It's amazing what God did over a meal, a rented office and a walk in the woods in Bumpus Mills, Tennessee. You may feel as though the circumstances and events that surround your life have no real value and are so obscure no one will ever notice. Do not ever think God isn't able to take something small and obscure and turn it into something that will touch the world for His glory. The key to it all is learning the difference between performing duties for God and having God inhabit your praise unto Him. With God nothing is impossible, even if it starts in Bumpus Mills, TN.

Prayer

My heavenly Father,

Great and mighty are Your works in the earth! I stand amazed at the wonders of Your faithful and masterful handiwork in my life. I marvel at the intricate patterns You have woven through the tapestry that makes up the days of my life. You have opened doors that no man could imagine and done wonders beyond my asking. Through it all You are masterfully establishing Your purpose and praise in this world. To consider how You chose to inhabit the womb of a virgin that one day I might have the hope of living eternally with You is more than my thoughts can grasp. To consider that You Who are perfectly righteous and full of the splendor of holiness chose to become sin that I might become the righteousness that is Yours alone is more than I will ever comprehend. I am presently imprisoned by finite thinking, but have the infinite Source of Life and Power living inside my heart. How is it You have chosen me to be the place of Your habitation? You are Great Jehovah, Redeemer, Mighty God, the risen Lamb Who is worthy of ALL my praise! You alone have silenced every accuser who would stand and otherwise rightfully accuse me of deeds that have the power to condemn me eternally. Yet, in perfect Love You are the Great Substitute Who has taken my sentence upon Yourself and placed Your robes of righteousness around my shoulders. As Your chosen son You have placed the signet ring of Your household upon my finger, removed the judgments against me and pardoned all my sin! Oh my God, I am so grateful and unworthy of such amazing love!!! When considering all You have done for me, how can I not in return give You every breath I breathe for the rest of my days? I am alive because of You! I have purpose because of You! I am pardoned because of You! No weapon formed against me can ever prosper because of You! I am more than a conqueror because of You! I am accepted in the Beloved because of You! My name is written in the Lamb's Book of Life because of You! Blessed be the name of the Lord! Bless the Lord O my soul! With all that I am and ever hope to be I proclaim and ascribe the glory due Your name. You are Great Jehovah, the Master and Captain of my soul! Great is the Lord! And greatly to be praised! Amen! Amen!

I will sing a new song to You, O God; On a harp of ten strings I will sing praises to You, The One who gives salvation to kings, Who delivers His servant From the deadly sword. Rescue me and deliver me from the hand of foreigners, Whose mouth speaks lying words, And whose right hand is a right hand of falsehood —
That our sons may be as plants grown up in their youth; That our daughters may be as pillars, Sculptured in palace style; That our barns may be full, Supplying all kinds of produce; That our sheep may bring forth thousands and ten thousands in Our fields; That our oxen may be well laden; That there be no breaking in or going out; That there be no outcry in our streets.
Happy are the people who are in such a state; Happy are the people whose God is the Lord!
Psalm 144:9-15

The Story Behind the Song:

What a perfect song to close this volume of thoughts, experiences and devotions from my life. God has truly proven to be a GREAT GOD in my life and His mercies toward me are GREATLY TO BE PRAISED! His love toward me continues to be GREAT! The debt I owed to Him for my rebellion and sin was GREAT, but His compassion toward me was even GREATER! His faithfulness throughout the days of my life has and always will be GREAT! His provision and protection in my life has been GREAT! His patience with me has been GREAT! His blessings toward me continue to be boundless and GREAT! He has honored and promoted me far beyond anything I deserve. His power and anointing in me has been and continues to be GREAT! His Word and His Voice through His blessed Holy Spirit have been my constant Guide, my continual Counselor, my Comfort in times of distress, my Joy in the midst of the journey, my Hope for the days ahead, and the sole Source of my praise, adoration and love. He truly is *Great Jehovah*, Mighty God, Redeemer and Deliverer of my soul. I love You, O Lord, my Rock my Strength, and my Song!

Great Jehovah

(Song from the Give Them Back project, music and lyrics written by Jerry Williams)

I've learned that no matter what comes
You'll always be there in Your strong and quiet presence
You lead me through each day of danger

Throughout all the days of my life
You've given Yourself that I might love You only
And know You as my Great Redeemer!

Chorus:
Great Jehovah! Almighty God!
The only Great Jehovah!
Fill my heart with all Your glory!
Jehovah! Redeemer, my Deliverer!
Great Jehovah!
I will praise and call You holy!

I remember the days of my youth
You promised if I would be true You'd always keep me
You've turned my loneliness to joy!

So often I started to run
But then You imparted Your love and tender mercies
You filled my nights with all Your glory!

Chorus

MINISTRY INFORMATION

EPIC Ministries, Inc.
PO Box 941388
Houston, Texas 77094
281-232-6922 Office
www.epicmnistries.org

Made in the USA
Columbia, SC
14 January 2022

53610297R00141